HOPE
in
Conflict

HOPE
in
Conflict

**Discovering Wisdom in
Congregational Turmoil**

David R. Sawyer

THE
PILGRIM
PRESS
Cleveland

For my mentors:
DANIEL B. WESSLER
W. BURNEY OVERTON
EDWIN H. FRIEDMAN

The Pilgrim Press, 700 Prospect Avenue
Cleveland, Ohio 44115-1100, U.S.A.
thepilgrimpress.com

© 2007 by David R. Sawyer

All rights reserved. Published 2007

❀ Printed in the United States of America on acid-free paper that contains
30% post-consumer fiber.

12 11 10 09 08 07 5 4 3 2 1

Library of Congress Cataloging-in-Publication Data

Sawyer, David (David R.)
    Hope in conflict : discovering wisdom in congregational turmoil /
David R. Sawyer.
        p. cm.
    Includes bibliographical references.
    ISBN 978-0-8298-1758-4 (alk. paper)
        1. Church controversies. 2. Conflict management – Religious aspects –
Christianity. 3. Church management. I. Title.
BV652.9.S24 2007
250 – dc22
                                                    2006036278

Contents

Preface

As a leader you know that a congregation can be wonderful and terrible, exciting and discouraging, nurturing and demanding, healing and hurting. You are familiar with the discouragement of disagreements, difficulties, or outright conflicts. If your experience is anything like mine, you have felt helpless and hopeless in the face of the mystery of a congregation that has emotionally blown up.

But hold on to that sense of mystery. If you are willing to live with mystery, study its hidden meanings, and perhaps even trust that God might be in that confusing uncertainty, you can find your way back onto the path to hope.

Naturalist and novelist Barbara Kingsolver tells of the hermit crab she brought home hidden in a shell she picked up on a vacation in the Caribbean. Since he was there, her family named him "Buster," made him a habitat-tank, fed him the best they could, and began a curious study of his unaccountable behavior patterns. The little crab lived up to the hermit image part of the time, and at other times entertained the family with startling hyperactivity. Kingsolver describes how she reflected on this mystery every morning while the coffee pot percolated beside Buster's tank. One of those mornings she remembered a reading from her graduate studies that unlocked the mystery. Animals who live in and around the seashore adapt themselves to the tides of their immediate habitat. Removed to the center of the continent, they adjust their cycles to the landlocked equivalents of the tides where they currently live. Even in a glass box in a suburban house in Tucson, Kingsolver decided, Buster was doing the best he could with what the world of her household was giving him.[1]

---

1. Barbara Kingsolver, *High Tide in Tucson: Essays from Now or Never* (New York: HarperPerennial, 1995), 6.

I believe that congregations are marvelous creatures, living eco-systems following their own inner principles and becoming their own unique selves. Hidden in each one is a distinctive mystery all its own. Each one deserves careful, loving, wise observation, in which the best knowledge of Bible, theology, history, and human nature are brought into conversation with the congregation's unique reality. This book invites you to that kind of loving and intentional investigation into the mystery of the hidden wisdom of your congregation. With the help of theology and social science concepts, you'll find here some concrete, easy-to-use tools to bring to light what is hidden, and an approach to appreciate that wisdom and to use it for good.

As a church leader, you are in a wonderful position to find hope hidden deep within a conflict. You can make a difference in moving a congregation to greater health. Here I define a leader as one who is willing to act from an inner sense of freedom and integrity and an outer demeanor of respectful communion with others to move the congregation's story into the future. Typically pastors are the leaders most centrally involved in leading a congregation through conflict, even though the pastor often is the focus of a conflict. While the ideas and practices I describe here are easily accessible by any church leader, they have particular resonance for a pastor struggling to find a way toward hope in difficult circumstances. Key lay leaders of the congregation, denominational contact persons, and outside consultants often also take leadership roles during congregational conflict. The reason I focus so much on hope and the possibility for change in this book is that above all I assume that God is at work in any and all conflicts in ways that we cannot fully grasp and surely cannot control. Because of this I invite you to join a humble partnership with the power of God. I firmly believe that a leader who is willing to look more deeply into this mystery can find hope in a conflicted situation in her or his church. No special expertise in conflict management or family systems theory is required for this hope to spring forth. But believing in the possibility takes some trust and both a perceptive and patient way of being.

My own experience with the worry and wisdom of conflict has led to this practical approach that I now call conflict utilization. I like "utilization" better than the more customary "conflict management" or "conflict resolution." The former suggests that it is possible to direct and control the outcome of a congregational conflict, and the latter hints at a possible simple solution to a complex set of relationships in a congregation. With "conflict utilization" I mean to suggest that the conflict itself presents an opportunity to imagine what God desires for the congregation's future. The hopeful leader sees the experience of conflict as an opportunity to unravel the clues in the deeper life of a congregation and to ask where God is working or trying to work in their midst. We can make the most of a conflict situation if we approach it as a mysterious and hopeful moment in the life of the congregation that requires our best spiritual, intellectual, and practical skills.

If you as a leader want to play a constructive role in the middle of a church conflict, you can find help in this model of conflict utilization. Listening for the deep message of goodness and health in the church, and loving the church and its members even at their most unlovely, can make a difference. Those who have learned this model have found that after a particularly emotional turn of events, sometimes following a sleepless night, the deeper wisdom of the situation springs to mind like a gestalt image, and the leader returns to a calmer, more optimistic attitude. Time after time the idea has been confirmed that, with this particular holistic approach, hope can be found in conflict, although it may be buried deep in a mound of confusion and emotion. Confident of the innate goodness and wisdom in the life of any congregation, you will be able to consider fresh ideas to encourage health and overcome a sense of despair. In most conflicts, a sense of hope is more important than the techniques for conflict management, or communication skills, although those are also useful.

In the chapters that follow we will explore and unravel the mystery of how to find hope hidden in the middle of conflict — your particular conflict. By all means move freely through the book. Read the chapters in a different order if you have a particular urgent concern, or if your learning style suggests it.

Chapter 1 introduces the problem of conflict in churches and describes how several of the current models of church conflict management would approach it. The contributions and limitations of these models are described in that chapter. Chapter 2 provides the initial steps a church leader takes to find hope in a conflicted situation. Chapters 3, 4, and 5 propose structures, stories, and symptoms as convenient ways to understand the mystery of your congregation's conflict. Chapter 6 introduces the use of a hopeful hypothesis as a way to seek positive health and to stay humble in the wake of conflict. Chapter 7 offers examples of concrete and workable strategies for bringing hope to bear on a congregational conflict by challenging the structures, stories, and symptoms in positive ways. In chapter 8, I describe the role of the pastor or other leader in conflict situations as "tapping the leader's inner sage." Chapter 9 shows how and why looking at structures, listening to stories, and learning from symptoms works to make conflict a hopeful, constructive experience for the congregation. I hope you will recognize the stories of congregations as being not so different from your own experience. I want them to help you find the hope that yours, too, does not need to remain stuck and conflicted.

Acknowledgments

The hope for the model of conflict utilization presented here was born in southeast Missouri with a group of volunteers who served as the conflict team for the Presbytery of Giddings-Lovejoy Committee on Ministry. I want to acknowledge and thank Ben Bradshaw, David Braun, Karen Blanchard, Deborah Fortel, Jerry Johnson, and Dick Neil, who studied structural[1] and strategic family systems theorists with me and served as a supervisory team for pairs of volunteers who were assigned to congregations in difficulty. The combined insights of that team resulted in significant progress toward improved health and strength in eleven of the fifteen seriously conflicted congregations during that period in the late 1980s. I owe much to my teachers in structural and systemic family therapy, Gene Colina of the Cincinnati Family Therapy Center and Ray Becvar of the St. Louis Family Institute. The concepts included here have been sharpened in consultations and workshops with congregational leaders across America in the past twenty years. Many of the concepts, originally borrowed from family theorists, have been shaped by my own interpretation and integration of the social scientific perspective with a practical theological perspective.[2] The stories are based on real experiences of colleagues and the congregations

---

1. For example, Salvador Minuchin and Charles Fishman, *Family Therapy Techniques* (Cambridge, MA: Harvard University Press, 1981), and Joel Bergman, *Fishing for Barracuda: Pragmatics of Brief Systemic Therapy* (New York: W. W. Norton, 1985).

2. For example the three key concepts in the book — looking at structures, listening to stories, and learning from symptoms — are borrowed from Salvador Minuchin: "The three strategies are challenging the symptom, challenging the family structure, and challenging the family reality," *Family Therapy Techniques*, 67. I have used the term "stories" instead of "reality" to provide an alliterative coherence to the strategies. For coaching pastoral leaders, I have found it helpful to think first of looking, listening, and learning to and from these clues before moving to strategies.

11

they have served, although I have altered the identities of people, places, and events for the sake of confidentiality.

For assistance in getting this book ready for you I gratefully acknowledge the wisdom and insight of my Pilgrim Press editor Ulrike Guthrie, the editorial support and encouragement of Janice Catron, the steady support and consideration of my Lifelong Learning Assistant, Carol Webb, my critical readers Sheri Ferguson, David Lowry, Pat and Earl Miller, Wayne Purintun, Julie Peterson, and the D. Min. Learning Group of Cindy Bean, Cynthia Brasington, Jack Copley, Harrell Davis, Altonnette Hawkins, Frank Johnson, and Kathy Keener-Han. The members of my Conflict Utilization class of Summer 2005, Bobbi Bella, Jeannie Harsch, Scot Hauser, Kathy McFall, Brenda McNair, Suellen Skinner, and Patricia Rivenbark, helped to focus and clarify the material. I thank the Louisville Presbyterian Theological Seminary for the encouragement of my faculty colleagues and for the sabbatical study time to prepare the manuscript. Special honor goes to my life-partner, Deborah Fortel, who co-created this model and who should be listed as the co-author of this book.

Chapter One

When a Key Is Not the Key

THE MYSTERY OF CHURCH CONFLICT

For some churches, conflict is a constant companion. In others, it erupts without apparent warning. In most of the churches experiencing conflict it hurts, it surprises, it eats away at the spiritual foundations of the members and leaders.

The eruption of conflict in your congregation should not be shocking or surprising. The mystery is what to do about it. Finding effective ways to manage and resolve conflict has eluded the church for centuries. I offer one of my own failures as an example. In my previous book I introduced a chapter on church conflict with this story.

Tempers had flared and friendships were strained. The governing board thought they might have to fire the pastor because members were so unable to work with him. Outside consultants were invited by the pastor and the board to help resolve the conflict. During the third meeting of the involved parties, the pastor turned to one of the women who was the most vocal and asked her what was upsetting her the most. She responded candidly that, when the recent remodeling of the church was completed, new locks were installed on some of the doors, and the officers of the women's organization were no longer able to get into the kitchen. The pastor immediately left the room. When he returned a few minutes later, he handed a kitchen key to the woman who had identified the underlying issue.

The group instantly dissolved into laughter of relief, and the task of the consultants was completed.[1]

Unfortunately, the story did not end there. The consultants, who were skilled in conflict management consulting techniques, packed up and went home, having done what they knew how to do. I only discovered much later that six months after that consultation the pastor was asked to leave the church. The first title of the story, as it was told in the paragraph copied here, was "the case of the kitchen key." Now I would title the story, "When a key is not the key" and take it as an example of the riddle of church conflict: What does it take to restore a squabbling, divided, emotionally charged congregation to wholeness?

The Pervasiveness of Church Conflict

Of course church conflict has been around a long time. The first group of Christians impressed their neighbors with the quality of their beloved community in the fourth chapter of Acts. All things were held in common, and love overcame self-interest in their life together. By chapter 6 of Acts, however, the scene had changed. The church had continued to grow and now included different ethnic groups. The administration of the Apostles as the servant-rulers of the community was challenged. Conflict erupted over the pastoral care and distribution of resources to the poorer members of the community, fueled by suspicion that the Greek-speaking segment of the community were not as well taken care of as those who spoke Aramaic. The organizational tradition, though still very young, was that all the teaching, all the pastoral care, and all the administration would be done by those originally appointed by Jesus. Inexplicably, holding onto that tradition only brought pain. In that first described conflict, the Apostles recommended a change in the church rules to

---

1. David Sawyer, *Work of the Church: Getting the Job Done in Boards and Committees* (Valley Forge, PA: Judson Press, 1986), 88.

allow differentiation of leadership roles with new leaders chosen to fairly represent the whole community for administrative service (Acts 6:1–6). That solved the first problem, but it did not end conflict in the church. Even Paul and his partner Barnabas (known as "Mr. Encouragement") ran into an unsolvable conflict with each other, and they broke the unity of the church to go their separate ways (Acts 15:36–40).

Contemporary theologians have noted the wide presence of church conflict. Amy Plantinga Pauw described the tensions in her own branch of the Protestant faith this way: "The self-righteous determination of Calvinists convinced they are doing God's will has few equals in the Christian tradition."[2] Commenting on the tendency of church members to fall into the culture's achievement-orientation, Craig Dykstra wrote that we become victims of our own win-lose mentality. He labeled this as "socially mutual self-destruction"[3] By way of further illustration, as this chapter is being composed, several major old-line denominations are on the brink of splitting over the issue of human sexuality. So far none of the solutions offered by committees and assemblies has diminished the conflict.

We can argue that the current climate of our culture has played a part in the phenomenon of congregational conflict. The ability of most people to engage in conversation around controversial topics has been diluted by the influences of television and radio talk shows in which "discussion" is presented as interrupting, shouting, and name-calling. Growing societal individualism has prompted people to react angrily to events and changes that might have been tolerated in the past. "Road rage" and "I'm out of here" have become common individualistic responses to tensions of life in community. No quick and easy solutions have come forward for that phenomenon, either.

---

2. Amy Plantinga Pauw, "The Church as a Community of Gift and Argument," unpublished work in progress, 2002.

3. Craig Dykstra, *Growing in the Life of Faith: Education and Christian Practices* (Louisville: Geneva Press, 1999), 86.

Trying Out Other Keys
to the Mystery of Conflict

You may already be aware of various approaches that offer keys to understanding church conflict. The ones I have found fall into three major categories: organization development, improvement of faith or communication, and family systems theory. I invite you to imagine yourself trying each of these keys to address and resolve the conflict in the Kitchen Key congregation.

The Organization Development Key

The consultants working with the Kitchen Key case operated on the theory and practice of organization development, sometimes called "organization*al* development," and usually referred to as "OD." Emerging in the mid-twentieth century from organizational psychology, OD made its way into church life as a new set of lenses for understanding how a church works. The OD conflict management methods relied heavily on direct communication in order to clarify expectations and negotiate fair outcomes among opposing factions or individuals in a church. This is why the consultants in the Kitchen Key case had gathered the leaders of the church in a series of meetings to get the conflict out in the open. It is also why they took the statements of the women's association leader and the action of the pastor at face value. They seemed to be breakthrough moments in the conflict and to represent true feelings and honest attempts at reconciliation.

Using the OD approach you could have charted the conflict resolution process through a decision tree that follows the logical progression of decisions and outcomes through to a successful conclusion. Halverstadt illustrates the use of a flowchart to pursue the resolution of conflict.[4] Susek uses a similar multiple step–method to approach church conflicts.[5] If the "Kitchen Key case" consultants had used these logical and direct methods, it is possible they might

---

4. Hugh F. Halverstadt, *Managing Church Conflict* (Louisville: Westminster John Knox, 1991).

5. Ron Susek, *Firestorm: Preventing and Overcoming Church Conflicts* (Grand Rapids, MI: Baker Books, 1999).

have prevented the congregation from falling back into win-lose power struggles that ultimately made the pastor bear the blame as the identified problem person for the underlying conflicts.

The OD method uses the problem solving methods of organizational science. You would probably find them helpful for problems that may be intense but are relatively simple. They are less likely to be effective in more complex and emotional situations. Organization Development approaches such as those of Leas, Halverstadt, and Susek, tend to fall short in two areas: (1) Because they assume that congregations are rational organizations, they do not take into account the deeper, hidden, emotional interrelationships at work in a congregation. (2) OD conflict management methods also tend to overlook the God question in favor of an assumption that God has delegated the organizational business of the church to reasonable, pragmatic people. They do not ask about what God might be doing in a congregation or in its surrounding community that has brought the congregation into the turmoil of the conflict.[6] For example, the OD consultants in the Church Key case could have raised questions about the declining vitality of the downtown area where the church building was located and asked what God might be calling the congregation to do to respond to those changes.

Communicational and Theological Keys

You may have tried using a type of conflict resolution that emphasized improving the communication in congregations. Some better communication might have prompted the Kitchen Key case to turn out somewhat differently.

If you were using George Thompson's work you would have urged the pastor and even the consultants to take more time building better relationships with the various groups of church members, getting to know the context of the situation, and creating the kind

---

6. Speed Leas, *Discover Your Conflict Management Style,* rev. ed. (Bethesda, MD: Alban Institute, 1997), and Halverstadt, *Managing Church Conflict,* are both excellent at asking theological and ethical questions, but they do not ask the more elusive transformational questions.

of foundation of relationships (what Thompson calls "cultural capital") that could weather some of the turbulence of conflict.[7] Without doubt many church leaders have fallen into unnecessary conflict because they either did not adequately understand the context of their situation or failed to build trust and confidence among the members of the church. It seems to me, however, that the pastor in the Kitchen Key case had already lost his opportunity to understand and relate deeply and well to his congregation.

If you had followed Marlin Thomas's practices you would have recommended a faith-oriented process of simple steps with biblical references to encourage better communication among the disputing members.[8] This might have caught the attention of some of the more traditionally minded members of the congregation and prompted them to act in more Christian ways. The Thomas methods are unfortunately prescriptive and may not take enough of the emotional and interactive context into account in finding a longer lasting solution to the problem than the OD consultants did.

From the perspective of Lloyd Rediger you probably would have quickly identified the presence of members of the congregation who were playing an antagonistic role toward the pastor.[9] This might have at least alerted you to the likely outcome that pressure would mount for the pastor to leave. This shifts the attention from the pastor as the identified problem person who is either universally blamed for the problems of the rest of the church or whose personal problems deflect the attention of the church from other issues of change or interrelated anxieties.[10] As you worked with Rediger's model, you would also have seen how his prescriptive or diagnostic approach short-circuited a fuller reflection on the church's problem. Naming the so-called clergy killers also would have avoided recognizing the

7. George Thompson Jr., *How to Get Along with Your Church: Creating Cultural Capital for Doing Ministry* (Cleveland: Pilgrim Press, 2001).

8. Marlin Thomas, *Resolving Disputes in Christian Groups* (Winnipeg: Windflower Communications, 2001).

9. Lloyd Rediger, *Clergy Killers: Guidance for Pastors and Congregations under Attack* (Louisville: Westminster John Knox, 1997).

10. See "Characters in Church Narratives" on page 64 for descriptions of the various interrelated roles people play in the church's story.

interrelationships of these roles and hindered a fuller understanding of God's desired changes in the church.

Family Systems Keys

If you had been influenced by the family systems movement, you might have tried to follow the lead of Edwin Friedman, who translated the Bowenian family systems model for church work.[11] Perhaps you also saw this approach in Peter Steinke's books, which developed a full consultation process for dealing with church conflict using those concepts.[12] Both Friedman and Steinke lead from Bowenian theory, which prompts you to focus on the levels of anxiety in the church, by (a) identifying the triangles among members and groups, (b) including those which place the pastor in the odd-one-out position, (c) seeking out the leaders in the congregation who could function at a less anxious or more self-differentiated way, and (d) encouraging them to work toward greater emotional health. If you had been reading Ron Richardson's books you might also have paid more attention to the ways the anger and the power plays in the Church Key congregation served as symptoms of unresolved difficulty in the church.[13] You would have noticed how the church functioned as an interrelated whole with tendencies toward either more closeness or more distance, and with functioning at more or less differentiated levels. You could recommend that members of the church study the ways of healthy functioning and work to change the anxious reactivity into more effective functioning.

Both Steinke's and Richardson's approaches to conflict attend in a useful way to the complex interconnectedness of congregations. In that sense you would have moved the consultation with the Kitchen Key church further along than the OD consultants or the communicational enhancers. However, from the Steinke and Richardson perspective, you might have failed to take the interconnectedness

---

11. Edwin Friedman, *Generation to Generation* (New York: Guilford, 1985).

12. Peter Steinke, *How Your Church Family Works* (Bethesda, MD: Alban Institute, 1993), and *Healthy Congregations* (Bethesda, MD: Alban Institute, 1996).

13. Ronald W. Richardson, *Creating a Healthier Church: Family Systems Theory, Leadership, and Congregational Life* (Minneapolis: Fortress, 1996), and *Becoming a Healthier Pastor* (Minneapolis: Fortress, 2004).

far enough to really acknowledge the full complexity of any given situation. The cause of the conflict would have been assumed to come in a linear fashion from the anxiety and lack of differentiation in the organization, and the solution would have been prescribed in that same linear way — eliminate the triangles and encourage a more objective, rational approach to the situations at hand.[14] I suspect that with Steinke and Richardson, you would have seen the Kitchen Key church case end with a pastoral exit, although the pastor might have been more prepared and ready to adapt to the new realities. Still the congregation might have missed a chance to address their unresolved turmoil over change and adapt to it.

A slightly different approach to family systems thinking is taken by Cosgrove and Hatfield.[15] By taking a far more active participation in the situation than the more objective Bowenian approach, you would likely have done a better job of connecting emotionally and openly with the Kitchen Key church than the OD consultants did (using the concept of joining the system). The full, circular complexity of the system is also explored with the structural mapping techniques presented in Cosgrove and Hatfield.[16] Mapping the interaction patterns and structures in the Kitchen Key church could have shed more light on the complexity and turmoil hidden behind the symptoms and words. The map might have shown unclear structures and inadequate role definitions, particularly for the pastor and for the church board. It might have shown some of the same people occupying several different offices and roles in the church structure, leading to some folks overfunctioning and others underfunctioning. Looking at a map could have revealed that the pastor and the women's fellowship had a rocky relationship for some time because of the pastor's positions on some social action issues in the community. Most significantly, a map could have shown the excess

---

14. Dorothy Stroh Becvar and Raphael J. Becvar, *Family Therapy: A Systemic Integration* (Boston: Allyn and Bacon, 2000), 167.

15. Charles H. Cosgrove and Dennis D. Hatfield, *Church Conflict: The Hidden Systems behind the Fights* (Nashville: Abingdon, 1994), who are more influenced by Salvador Minuchin than the Bowenian theories of family systems.

16. See chapter 3 of this book for more on mapping the structures of a congregation.

of power held by the board of trustees, which oversaw the reno-
vation process, along with a longstanding conflicted relationship
between the families of the chair of the board of trustees and the
president of the women's association. Without understanding these
structural imbalances, the conflict was doomed to continue to the
painful departure of the pastor.

Cosgrove and Hatfield's approach to congregational conflict represents a refreshing addition but it falls short of plumbing the full
mystery of church conflict. While following the main thrust of the
structural branch of the family systems movement, they left out
Minuchin's emphasis on stories and symptoms.[17] The congregation's stories are often windows into the active movement of God
in the congregation, and they indicate the openness to the future
that God desires for them.[18] The symptoms are more likely to point
to the changes happening around and in the congregation and the
turmoil that comes from either resisting the change or reacting to it.

Hunches about the Keys
to the Mystery of Conflict

If your experience is anything like mine, after trying some of these
other models you might still be searching for keys to unlock the
mystery of congregational conflict. As you begin to see how things
are interconnected in a whole system and start to recognize how
God is calling a congregation to be transformed, you are closer to
unlocking the puzzle.

In the twentieth century we tended to think of conflict in mostly
human terms. Either it was a human problem brought on by human

---

17. The reader should note that it is my own reading of Minuchin that empha-
sizes stories and symptoms alongside structures. Many other writers focus only on
the structural side of Minuchin's work. In *Family Therapy Techniques* (Cambridge,
MA: Harvard University Press, 1981), Minuchin and Fishman include chapters on
"Reframing" and "Realities." In these chapters they use the term "story" to refer
to the "therapeutic reality" of the family (73–74), but it is not the primary way of
expressing their point. My reframing of Minuchin's work around stories is based
on the practical helpfulness of narrative approaches to unraveling the mysteries of
church conflict. See the epigraph to chapter 4 (page 55) and note 3 on page 58.

18. See chapter 4 for a full discussion of listening to stories.

sin, or even evil, or it was a management problem to be solved with the most rational methods. New insights in human and natural sciences suggest that we need to begin to ask the question of where God is in all of this conflict.[19] By this I don't mean an "if all else fails, ask the God question." Rather, I mean let's draw on the twenty-first-century reawakening of spiritual sensitivities, both inside and outside the church. In our era it is not enough to simply assume the presence or absence of God and then move ahead to put our best thought to a church problem. I assume that God's involvement in the world is the continuing transformation of the world for personal growth and for the change that comes from creative interaction in the human community.[20] Therefore I suggest that in tackling church conflict we have to take change into account, and particularly the changes God desires for the church. I further assume that God created human beings for community and called Christians to be in a church community. Thus any thinking about church life has to take into account the communal nature of the church and the ways people relate to each other. This theological perspective fits nicely with current thinking about how the world works, from both natural and human sciences findings. A full understanding of what's going on requires a view of how everything is interrelated.

My hunches about church conflict flow from these theological and theoretical insights. First, I have a hunch that no theory of church life is sufficient without an understanding of the *interconnectedness* of the various complex factors of a church's life.[21] And second I have a hunch that an adequate approach to church conflict must account for *change*. No single key will unlock the complex mystery. The three strategies described in succeeding

---

19. Frederick Schmidt, *What God Wants for Your Life: Finding Answers to the Deepest Questions* (New York: HarperCollins, 2005).

20. John B. Cobb, *Reclaiming the Church: Where the Mainline Church Went Wrong and What to Do about It* (Louisville: Westminster John Knox, 1997), 60.

21. I use the terms "interconnectedness" and "interrelatedness" alternately to refer to the larger and sometimes confusing concepts of "systems" referring to the networks of relationships that characterize complex, self-organizing organisms, including human organizations. The first term is borrowed from Margaret Wheatley, *Finding Our Way: Leadership for an Uncertain Time* (San Francisco: Berrett-Koehler, 2005), 204ff.

chapters — structures, stories, and symptoms[22] — have opened for me the deeper mysteries of change and connectedness. I propose that we try them as keys in several cases of church conflict to try to unlock the mystery of conflict.

By reflecting on the story of Jesus feeding the five thousand we can put connection and change into perspective. In Mark 6:30ff, Jesus and the twelve were tired and hungry. They had not been able to take their Sabbath rest because the crowd had followed them and Jesus had taken compassion on the crowd. As the afternoon passed into the evening, the twelve began to think about a way to meet the needs of everybody — Jesus, themselves, and the crowd. As part of their responsibility for the Rabbi's learning group, they had brought enough food for themselves. The simplest and most immediate solution was to send everyone else away to seek food and shelter, and then Jesus and the twelve could rest and eat.

When they presented the plan to Jesus, he challenged their solution and instructed them to reflect further on the situation and to use the resources at hand to feed the crowd. His words, "You give them something to eat," sound abrupt and unreasonable. The rest of the story in the form of a miracle narrative supports the hunches I've made about addressing the mystery of conflict in congregations. Jesus asks the twelve to step back and reflect further not only on their resources, but on two other factors they had not considered. First, that they themselves and the people gathered around them constituted a community of faith, an interrelated, living organization. They were not singularly or solely responsible for meeting the needs of that vast group of people, counted as five thousand men. Second, they had not allowed for the possibility that God could be using this situation as a transforming moment. Things need not always be what they always were. A new reality can emerge from a crisis of hunger and need. The feeding of the five thousand is a lesson of no quick fixes. It taught the early church, if not the twelve apostles, to look for the connections of their lives together and to expect God to work wonderful changes among the mysteries of life.

---

22. Minuchin and Fishman, *Family Therapy Techniques,* 67.

Chapter Two

Looking, Listening, and Learning

SERVING AS A LEADER WHEN CONFLICT EMERGES

Valerie and Edwin Bradford were feeling very good about the state of their congregation and its pastor. Antioch Presbyterian Church had a one-hundred-year history of ministry in the center of their home city, and Pastor Joe Freeman had arrived two years earlier to help the congregation make the transition from its historic ministry to a vibrant engagement with the needs of the immediate neighborhood. In keeping with their family tradition, Valerie and Edwin had become Joe's staunch supporters as he worked to revitalize the worship at Antioch and to create a homeless shelter, using grants and funding from many sources to remodel the church building into a hospitable place with a commercial kitchen, sleeping rooms, and bathing facilities. It was an exciting time to be part of Antioch Church!

Those good feelings turned to worries when they began hearing of a campaign of complaints about Pastor Freeman circulating among the congregation. People were angry that their church building was being taken over by the poorest and possibly most dangerous people in the neighborhood. They were also upset that the worship that had brought them such pride and comfort through the years had changed. Edwin and Valerie quickly met with Joe to find out how he was responding to these complaints. They discovered that he was angry and defiant, insisting that his vision was correct and adamant about his right to act out his vision as the pastor of Antioch Church.

Back home in their kitchen after meeting with Joe, the Bradfords struggled with their initial despair that their beloved church might be splintered by a destructive conflict. As young professionals they knew enough about how organizations work to recognize the danger. As people of faith they were also aware that something more mysterious was at work here beneath the human drama. They reminded each other that God would not be absent in this moment of crisis, but could, in fact, be working in and perhaps through the crisis in Antioch Church. That thought reassured them that the burden of this conflict did not rest solely on them nor indeed solely on the pastor. The congregation as a body was likely to have the resources and resilience to weather this storm and move forward in faith. What they wanted was to prepare themselves, the pastor, and the other members to address this mystery with all the resources and resilience of their beloved congregation.

Getting Started as Leaders

Although your church conflict situation presents its own unique challenges, be reassured that your initial responses to it as a leader usually entail fairly straightforward choices and possibilities, including choosing to lead, prayerful discernment, inviting others to collaborate, creating a team, covenanting for a clean conflict process, and deciding whether and when to bring in outside assistance. I hope this book will encourage you to choose to be a leader in conflict, defined here as *one who acts from an inner sense of freedom and integrity and an outer demeanor of respectful communion with others to move the congregation's story into the future.*[1]

I invite you to compare and contrast your situation to that of the Antioch Church as its leaders made choices and found hopeful starting points in their difficult situation.

Prayerful Discernment about Taking a Role of Leadership

Both Joe Freeman and the Bradfords faced immediate choices in this situation. Three obvious alternatives presented themselves: to

---

1. See the character roles in chapter 4 (pages 62ff.) and a full description of wise, mature leadership in chapter 8.

fight, flee, or lead. Depending on personal preferences, emotional involvement, and spiritual foundation, a case can be made for any of the three.

Before making that choice, however, Joe, Valerie, and Edwin had to stop and reflect about their own motivation and commitment in taking a lead. They wisely recognized that they needed to be able to prayerfully discern whether they could honestly hold on to their own freedom and integrity while allowing the congregation to take full responsibility to turn the conflict from chaos into hope. They also needed to ask themselves whether they would be able to trust their congregation to God's transforming spirit in the process of dealing with conflict.

Two discernment questions were uppermost in the minds of this pastor and these lay leaders. First, they asked for guidance to clarify their own inner motives in the situation. Like many pastors (and members and outside consultants) Joe felt strongly that he had to respond to this conflict out of a sense of responsibility to fix or to save the church from the conflict. Getting clear about these inner motivations helped him realize that he was far too invested in his own agenda for this congregation and probably too intent on "winning" the fight to able to play a helpful leadership role. After he learned about the rising complaints, he had struggled to find the strength in himself to love and care for the congregation and all of its members. He was not sure he could fully act out what he knew to be his best self, but he knew he needed two particular inner qualities if he was going to see this conflict through: an openness to the leading of the Spirit of God in the situation, and respect for the choices of the congregation to settle the conflict in whatever way it worked out. His own need to win and his reaction to others' criticisms would continue to compete in his own heart with his desire to help his congregation find its inner wisdom, and to allow the congregation to assume its own responsibility.

The second discernment question is similar but takes a different tack. In approaching this conflict Joe was forced to ask himself if he was indeed more committed to truth and God's will in this matter than to his own personal agenda or viewpoint. Conflict often arises when things are changing or when God wants change to happen in a congregation. Out of his own vision, not fully shared with the people, Joe had pushed the congregation to change. Now the congregation was reacting and resisting. Reluctantly, Joe recognized that he would have trouble giving up his agenda for change in that congregation.

Fortunately Edwin and Valerie loved both Joe and their congregation enough to ask the same discernment questions for themselves. They were excited to take on the challenge of leadership though saddened by the conflict itself and their pastor's heavy involvement in it. Nonetheless, they believed they could do some things to help their congregation move beyond its difficulties. At the same time, they believed they had enough emotional distance from the situation to look fairly and clearly at the various points of view and to ascertain God's leading for the best way to move this congregation to greater strength and wholeness.

When Joe met with Valerie and Edwin the second time, they agreed that Joe would step aside from any key leadership role in addressing the conflict and instead ask them to take the lead in bringing the matter to other church leaders. This decision was based on the unique situation of Antioch Church and is not necessarily recommended for all situations. It is offered here as an example of how leaders can use careful discernment and make wise choices in difficult situations.

Inviting Conflicted Individuals or Groups to a Conversation

A leader has to have conversation partners in order to make a difference in any organization. For the leaders of Antioch Church, finding partners was not a simple task.

Since complaints had already circulated around the congregation, no attempt to keep the conflict quietly behind the scenes would succeed. Based on a belief that a conflict about mission and priorities and leadership directions belongs to the whole congregation and not just to a few insiders, Edwin and Valerie, with Joe's permission, began to talk openly about the growing trouble with key members

of the church. They identified some of the people who were participating in the informal communication networks. They knew where
they had heard about it, and they also theorized about others who
were likely participants in that movement. They also openly mentioned the concerns to other members who were enthusiastic about
Joe's leadership, and who supported either the new style of worship
or the homeless shelter.

Together they agreed on a three-part approach to each person.
First, they introduced the topic of the conflict, being careful to speak
about their own personal knowledge and feelings rather than talk
about others. Second, they used their best listening skills with each
person to hear what she or he had to say about it. After actively
listening, if it seemed appropriate, they asked that person if he or
she would be open to participating in further conversations with
others with the hope that everyone could learn more about what
the conflict was about and what it meant. Some people were either
so angry or so shocked that they were not willing to have further
open conversations. Some were not even aware of the conflict and
were not particularly interested. Most of Edwin and Valerie's conversations, however, led to a willingness to discuss the differences
people were having with each other. They could tell fairly readily
from the responses to their initial presentation whether the person
was going to be a helpful participant in the process or not. The fact
that they encouraged each of their conversation partners to have
similar informal calm and hopeful conversations with others kept
the issue from becoming a more divisive matter of taking sides or
keeping secrets. They also gathered a list of people on differing sides
of the issues who expressed willingness to attend a meeting to have
further discussion.

Creating a Congregational Conflict Task Force

With early conversations under way it is typically helpful to establish an official group of people who can guide the leaders and the
congregation through the muddy waters of the conflict. The Antioch
situation provides an example of how that can be done.

Since Valerie was on the church board, she agreed with Joe and Edwin that she would raise the subject at an upcoming meeting. Again she would be careful to be fair and hopeful in her message to the board. The meeting was tense at first. When it was clear to the group that Pastor Freeman was comfortable with such conversation, the board members were able to acknowledge that there was trouble brewing and that they needed to take some responsibility for the health of the congregation. They followed Valerie's recommendation to create a small task force, accountable to the board, to work with Joe and the congregation to address the conflict. Wise members who were respected and trusted in the congregation at large, who were willing to approach the subject fairly and calmly, and who represented differing viewpoints on the issues in the conflict were named and recruited to guide the congregation through the immediate future of putting the conflict into some constructive framework.

The task force met with the pastor first to keep communication open with him. Then they met separately to begin to plan ways to use the conflict to bring the church to greater faithfulness and health. After their first meeting they selected additional members for listening and gathering more information.

As you expect in your own situation too, not everything went smoothly at Antioch. While those conversations were going on, a letter was unfortunately circulated among a segment of the congregation seeking to get rid of the pastor. At the next church board meeting, Joe Freeman brought out the letter and gave an angry speech to the board about his prerogative as pastor of an African American congregation to set the leadership direction and to direct the worship life of the church. He declared that the congregation had called him to be their pastor and no small group of members was going to force him to leave or to give up his vision for that church. He went so far as to threaten that if he left the congregation would surely die. The members of the church board were so stunned by his outburst that they could not immediately find a way to respond as a group. Members of the board began to argue with each other about whether the pastor was right or the complainers were right. When the meeting finally adjourned, Valerie called her husband, Edwin, and they met with Pastor Freeman at the coffee shop near the church. Joe was so angry that he had lost his hope for a constructive resolution to this situation. He felt he was ready to fight the complainers to the end. The Bradfords were sorry that he had reacted so strongly. They offered him their concern and support, but they restated their desire to find a way to bring hope to a hopeless situation. Before they left that evening, the three of them were able to agree that the conflict team should consider inviting the denomination's regional executive to help them address these problems.

Deciding to Bring In Outside Help

In an ideal world, every congregation would have a support network of denominational or associational colleagues with a system for responding to church conflict. In such a world, a call to the denominational office would prompt a response from a conflict team that knows the difference between fixing conflict and finding hope in the midst of conflict. As a leader, you can determine whether in your own situation you can anticipate an ecclesiastical relationship with denominational officers who would appreciate an early notice of difficulties without necessarily insisting on intervening. Such a healthy relationship could lead to supportive understanding and coaching when needed in a difficult situation.

The leaders at Antioch Church knew that their denominational office had a team specially designated to respond to congregational conflict, so they could weigh the choice of calling in outside help with some confidence in that resource. The heavy emotionality of the last meeting, and Pastor Freeman's anger and sense of professional entitlement seemed to place him, at least for the moment, beyond taking a constructive leadership role in addressing the conflict. The anxiety that his outburst spread among the board members showed that most of them were as caught up in the issues as their pastor. The task force had to ask themselves whether they would be able to create an atmosphere of hope and calm soon enough to prevent further escalation of the difficulties. After a full discussion with time for prayer, they found themselves lacking in adequate responses to the situation and desiring the help of the denominational team. They also considered three other possibilities for outside assistance:

♦ A local psychotherapist who did organizational consulting with African American companies and not-for-profit agencies in the community. The task force gave this option less consideration because they did not have enough confidence that this person could translate secular methods into a church situation.

♦ The pastor of the largest African American congregation in the region, located in another city, who was a mentor of Pastor Joe and was considered to be a person of authority and influence who could bring a spiritual and pastoral approach to their problems. This received strong consideration in the early part of the conversation, but the task force worried that members of the church would perceive this minister as siding with the Rev. Freeman.

♦ One of the out-of-town organizations with a good reputation for congregational consulting, particularly in conflict situations. Initial inquiries with two of these organizations indicated that the fee schedules were too burdensome for Antioch Church's budget.

The task force decided[2] that Pastor Freeman would be asked to make the call to the denominational executive and request help from the team in order to keep lines of communication clear between Joe and the ecclesiastical network. The executive sent to Joe a written description of the conflict team's work and objectives and asked that the congregation's conflict task force take a recommendation to the church board formally asking for the help of the team. A special meeting of the board accomplished that action within a week.

---

2. Note that the choice of an outside consultant was unique to Antioch Church. In fact, these four options including the denominational team if in place are all worthy of consideration, depending on the context of the particular congregation.

Establishing Ground Rules
for Addressing Conflict

Among the early jobs of the congregation's conflict task force or the outside consultants is to encourage congregational members involved in the situation to allow each other a fair chance to share their thoughts and feelings in a safe environment. One way of doing this is to identify and achieve general agreement on some ground rules for running meetings. In the box on the following page I propose a set of six rules that a group might wish to adopt for keeping the conflict "clean" and fair. Each of these is based on good communication practices and faithful relationships in congregations.

A congregation may have its own set of guidelines for times of trouble, or it may wish to spend time early in the conflict coming up with a mutual covenant that receives a consensus among those participating. If the situation is highly volatile, and if the task force or outside team has sufficient credibility, suggesting items for the covenant something like those listed here can be a convenient shortcut. As the discussion of the issues of the conflict itself develops, the moderator of the meetings or members of the task force can help a group or meeting keep on track by calling individuals accountable to these guidelines. During meetings to discuss the conflict issues when things seem to get confused, bogged down, or out of control, a helpful intervention by moderators or others monitoring the process is to go back to review the covenant or ground rules. In those moments a reminder of such a covenant can be helpful. Sometimes adopting a new ground rule not thought of earlier can help get through the current impasse.

Presenting Issues and Deeper Realities

After identifying some conversation partners and establishing some ground rules for the conversation, the wise leader can begin to sort through the muddle of topics and issues to identify which are the presenting issues and what are the deeper realities in the conflict.

EXAMPLE OF GROUND RULES
FOR ADDRESSING CONFLICT

1. Listen to each other and "say it back." Before parties can rebut an opponent's statements, they must first repeat the statement in their own words.

2. Stick to the issues and stay away from personalities.

3. Stick to the present; do not bring up past conflicts.

4. The best offense is a good defense. State clearly your own position rather than attacking an opposing position.

5. If your position prevails, thank God. If your position is defeated, accept the majority decision and be patient.

6. Remember that it is Christ's church, not yours or mine, and we are seeking God's will first.

From David Sawyer, *Work of the Church: Getting the Job Done in Boards and Committees* (Valley Forge, PA: Judson Press, 1986), 95ff.

The troubles that were brewing at Antioch Church focused on the actions and style of the pastor, Joe Freeman. His critics claimed that he had changed the worship style at Antioch. For decades Antioch had practiced a very dignified liturgy, with music chosen from either the great African American spirituals, European classical music, or the predominately European hymnody of their mostly white denomination. He had introduced his own preferences in worship, including contemporary black gospel music and a more emotional informality designed to appeal to the younger residents of the community around the church building.

Joe had been called to Antioch with the specific charge to find ways to minister to that neighboring community. Within a few months of his arrival he had applied for and received major grants to do much-needed remodeling of the church building, updating the kitchen to commercial standards, and adding locker rooms with showers in order to establish a homeless shelter. The shelter program and building changes had been approved by the church board but were bitterly opposed by several key leaders in the congregation. It was the presence of the homeless people in the church building that prompted the largest outcry of protest from the older members of the church.

The denominational team heard the complaints of groups of members about worship and about the homeless shelter. The loudest voices they heard were those who blamed the church's problems on Joe and who sought to either change his approach or get him to leave. The level of anger and the degree to which the problems were attributed primarily to Joe provided the first opportunity to think about interconnectedness and change in the life of the congregation. On the face of it, the "simple" solution to the problems would have been to force Joe to change his worship style and close the homeless shelter, but a simple solution would have been neither simple nor a solution.[3] Just as a good counselor knows that the first "problem" presented by a client or family is typically only the client's way into a larger set of problems that lie beneath the surface, so a conflict team learns to sift through the clues and symptoms as presented to find the deeper and more difficult realities that have brought the "presenting problem" to the foreground right now.

A Period of Observation:
Looking, Listening, and Learning

Before drawing any conclusions about the nature of the situation, the conflict team needed to do careful gathering of information about how this church functions as an interconnected whole, and about what changes are taking place in their congregation and in its neighborhood.

Some guidelines for that period of observation are:

---

3. "Simple Solutions are an oxymoron." See Margaret Wheatley, *Finding Our Way* (San Francisco: Berrett-Koehler Publishers, 2005), 64.

1. The team will assume a posture of partnership and learning with the parties in the conflict, assuring fairness and even-handedness, and also holding a clear sense of its role as representing the denominational governing body as counselors, mediators, and/or interveners.

2. The team will lay out a plan for meeting with pastors, educators, elders, and a personnel committee to look at the way the church has organized itself around the conflict, to listen to the stories people tell about the church's situation, and to learn from the symptoms that are evident.

3. If the team deems them helpful, meetings or interviews with other groups or individuals may proceed after the initial meetings with the core leadership of the congregation.

Often the observation period can also serve as a "cooling off" period for the congregation.[4]

The chapters that follow outline an approach to gathering information about the congregation by looking at structures, listening to stories, learning from symptoms, and finding hope through the inner wisdom of a conflicted congregation.

"Behold, I Am Doing a New Thing"

As for how things turned out for Antioch Church: Joe Freeman and his friends Valerie and Edwin Bradford were not perfect, but they chose wisely in the ways they approached the conflict in their congregation. It was not easy, but the story turned out better than many. Their willingness to seek truth in a larger sense and transcend the temptation to win short-term battles in a fight for important principles of mission and justice helped them to see the underlying patterns woven into the life of their congregation. Eventually it became clear that the changes in the neighborhood and the changes in their own congregation over time had indeed led to a call to learn

---

4. If the conflict escalates during this time of observation, that becomes another piece of information on the function of the difficulty.

some new ways of being church together. While the early solutions that Joe had tried were not universally appreciated, they served as catalysts for learning that business as usual was not going to work anymore.

The turning point in the turmoil of conflict at Antioch Church came later that year on Easter Day. Reflecting on the resurrection texts of the glorious music of the choir and the soloists that Sunday, Joe presented a different kind of an Easter sermon that day. He talked openly of his struggles with the way things were and his own skepticism about whether something good or new could come of the difficulties. He admitted that he himself had resisted the spirit of cooperation that was required to turn the chaos of conflict into a new and better chapter in the life of the church. Then he offered an imagined resurrection story that came to him as he was preparing his message for that day.

> One afternoon as a group of disciples were traveling through a deserted area, a thunderstorm drenched them. Taking shelter in an overhanging cave near the road they waited out the storm until after nightfall. With their wet firewood they could not get a fire going to protect them from the cold and the wild animals. Tired, afraid, confused by the crucifixion and skeptical about the stories of resurrection sightings, they fell back into their old ways of bickering and blaming. After a period of arguing they fell silent.
>
> Then, without a word one of them laid on the fire bed a small bundle of dry wood he had been saving for a family celebration back home. Another of their number pulled from her robes a vial of oil that she used for anointing those who came to her for advice and healing. With a glance at the others with whom she had quarreled, she poured the oil on the wood. A third disciple moved quickly to strike the flint to ignite the fire.
>
> As the flames rose, lighting faces around the fire, they realized that Jesus was sitting among them watching them with love in his eyes. In the light of his love their fear vanished, their doubts evaporated, and they knew they were changed

forever. And Jesus said, "Truly I tell you, the day is coming soon when your church will burst into tongues of fire, fueled with self-sacrificing love, ignited by the energy of faith, and fanned by the changing winds of the Spirit. Behold I am doing a new thing."

The path from that Easter Sunday was not an easy one for Antioch Church or for Pastor Joe Freeman and his friends. But it was a different journey than they might have taken because they had recognized the presence of the risen Christ among them, changing them from being afraid, angry, skeptical, and needing to win at all costs. As the conflict task force worked with new eyes and an appreciation for God's changes, the leaders of that congregation discovered anew the energy to look at how they organized themselves, to listen for their stories, and to learn from the new things God placed before them. They found hope in the midst of their conflict, and Antioch Church is a better congregation because they did.

Reflection on Serving as a Leader When Conflict Emerges

1. No matter how urgent and compelling the pull to move quickly toward resolving your situation, take some time to identify possible first steps to establish a foundation for finding hope in your congregation.

2. Prayerfully ask yourself what your role is in the situation and whether you are prepared, willing, and able to serve as a leader in this particular situation. Honestly ask if you are motivated to play either a savior or a victim role. Ask for some help with these questions from a trusted friend who is not directly involved in the conflict.

3. Start a list of members of your congregation who would be constructive conversation partners to address the issues of this conflict.

4. Consider what outside resources are available to your congregation, and prepare to do some networking or research to find outside partners who could assist you and your congregation.

5. Name at least one "presenting" issue in the conflict, and then write your best guess about what deeper reality in your congregation's life might lie behind the presenting issue. You can come back to this note after you have worked through chapters 3 through 6 to check your guess in light of the information you have gathered.

Chapter Three

Looking at Structures

MAPPING THE PATTERNS
OF A CONGREGATION IN CONFLICT

The inventor Buckminster Fuller was fond of holding up his hand and asking people, "What is this?" Invariably, they would respond, "It's a hand." He would then point out that the cells that made up that hand were continually dying and regenerating themselves. What seems tangible is continually changing: in fact, a hand is completely re-created within a year or so. So when we see a hand — or an entire body or any living system — as a static "thing," we are mistaken. "What you see is not my hand," said Fuller. "It is a 'pattern integrity,' " the universe's capacity to create hands.[1]

An observer of a work of art in a museum sees a "picture" as an instantaneous whole. Yet our appreciation of that work is increased, and the whole is enhanced by noting line and color, design and illusion. In a like manner, the observer of an organization such as a congregation focuses on the interpersonal architecture, frameworks, arrangements, composition, and other categories of order to gain a greater appreciation of the overall meaning of that organization. To interpret the truth of any organization, and in our case, of a church, as an observer we must look for the patterns in the ways the group has come together and defined themselves.

---

1. Quoted in Peter Senge and others, *Presence: An Exploration of Profound Change in People, Organizations, and Society* (New York: Currency Books, 2004), 6.

A congregational leader seldom has the luxury of being an observer. Whether you are a member, a leader, or a consultant, identifying patterns of behaviors is necessary and helpful to understand the underlying dynamics of how we live together and what is really going on. Because a congregation's ways of being together often operate beyond awareness, identifying patterns of interrelationship and change makes it possible for one's participation to be healthy and transformative for both oneself and the congregation. In this chapter we look at structures as the first way of seeing and interpreting the clues of congregational conflict.

Trouble in Big Bluff City Church

In the case of the Big Bluff City Church, a four-hundred-member congregation in a medium-sized town built on the cliffs overlooking a river, the anger and the blaming were preventing the pastor and most of the lay leaders from looking at their congregation as an interrelated organism with hope for change and growth.

The afternoon that Annabelle Shackelford phoned Agnes, the denominational regional minister, Annabelle launched into a long list of complaints against her pastor at the Big Bluff City Church. Presenting herself as a very committed church member who spoke for the majority of the congregation, she reported that members were leaving because the congregation was angry with Pastor Percy Noble. Percy was not doing his work, she claimed. He had not called on dear Aunt Helen, for example, when she had been so sick. He showed up just before she died, but where had he been before that? Noble's sermons were radically leftist in outlook, she complained, giving people political rhetoric when they needed consolation and peace from their church. These concerns and many more tumbled out in an uninterruptible hour-long torrent of emotion. Annabelle finished the phone call by stating that she wanted someone to come in and "do something about this terrible situation." Agnes offered to look into the matter and get back to her.

When Agnes called Rev. Noble to inquire about these concerns, Noble responded with an outburst that matched Annabelle's for emotion. He said he had been harassed for the past two years by what he perceived to be a small group of church members. He had reasonable explanations for each of the incidents she reported. He noted that criticisms from his detractors had increased sharply since his recent heart attack. From his point of view there was another list of horrors inflicted on him and the rest of the church by that group. For example, they had created a so-called evangelism committee — which had spent its time and efforts visiting inactive members and asking them to document what they did not like about the pastor. Noble felt so threatened by the group of complainers that he had not taken a vacation away from town in several years, fearing they might mount a successful campaign to fire him while he was gone.

Following denominational policy, Agnes invited Bill, a member of the conflict team of the region, to accompany her to a series of meetings at Big Bluff Church. They met with the angry group who had complaints against the pastor, and they met with a fearful and somewhat rebellious Rev. Noble. In two "listening meetings" with the church board, Agnes and Bill observed that the board members appeared to be divided into camps for and against the pastor, contrary to what Annabelle had suggested. At the same time, the board members were not very familiar with the powers and responsibilities of their position on the board. Most of the standing committees were not functioning, and several board members had no committee assignments whatever. Rev. Noble acknowledged that, intimidated by the more vocal complaining group, he had refused to allow the board to make substantive decisions about the life of the congregation. Some board members indicated that they were also being harassed and intimidated by members of the group opposed to the pastor, represented by Annabelle. Leaders of that group expected (and received from their supporters) full reports about what was said by whom and how in board meetings.

Nonetheless, there was evidence of strength among the board members. Two or three of them admitted that they thought the conflict was more about changes in the community and in the church than it was about any alleged misbehavior by the pastor. They reported that the neighborhood around the church was undergoing a demographic shift, and crime was rising in the area. Many of them expressed anxiety about how they would be able to keep their church going when things were changing all around.

The task of the regional minister and the conflict team was to help Big Bluff City Church, its leaders, and its pastor to move beyond the anger and fears that kept them in turmoil and to find a common sense of identity and mission. At first glance, it appeared to be hopeless, and they feared that the conflict would only accelerate and that the pastor would not be able to continue in ministry in that congregation.

Looking at the Structures of Big Bluff City Church

To make sense of the painful situation, the conflict team reviewed the structures of the congregation. This tactic helped them see the whole picture of the situation and find hope and health in a troubled congregation.

So we see that in the middle of a congregational conflict, leaders who remember to look at structures, at the big picture, at the whole situation, will more easily think of the congregation as an interrelated whole and thus identify the community's patterns of organization for health or for hardship, rather than pointing the finger at individuals and their faults. Looking for patterns in organizational structures is also the place to start to find hope. It is the easiest and simplest tool you need to understand what's going on. As we see in the case of Big Bluff City, sometimes the simplest structural assessment and intervention can make the difference between destructive conflict and healthy transformation of a congregation.

Over the years, like any group of people, the congregation of Big Bluff City Church have organized themselves with a unique and observable set of patterns. The most obvious structures are the board, the committees of the church, and the professional staff headed by Percy. Other parts were identified such as the choir, the Sunday school, and the women's organization. Besides these formal structures, two informal subunits were readily identifiable. First was the group of people who had come together in opposition to their pastor. The other group, perhaps not as obvious or as vocal, but notable by their representation on the church board, was the group that supported Percy's ministry among them.

Seeing Rules and Roles

It helps to see how the patterns of subsystem or component parts of a system are created and maintained through the rules and roles by which they function.[2] These rules and roles can be formal or informal, and they also can be explicit or implicit. The Big Bluff City church board had formal rules printed in the congregation's constitution requiring it to meet on a regular basis, and regulating the way business was to be conducted, for example, by Robert's Rules of Order. The roles of the chairperson of the board and the secretary and the treasurer of the organization were also formally defined in the rules. Informally, however, the officers and members of the board at Big Bluff tended to defer to the pastor for direction on the kinds of decisions to make. Informally, the pastor was able to keep important decisions from coming to the board at all and could therefore also prevent the board from making potentially divisive choices about issues of the church simply by not letting them know about some specific things. The roles of the members of the board, while spelled out in the constitution, were not well defined in practice. The role of the pastor was also not clearly understood; he was seen as doing too much in his power over the board and doing too little in his lack of caring for members. In fact it would be safe to say that at Big Bluff City Church there were disagreements about the role the pastor played in the congregation. Some were happy with the pastor playing a dominant role on the board and speaking out on controversial issues of the day. Others defined the role of pastor as being primarily to give comfort and nurture to the congregation and to those who are sick.

---

2. Kenneth Mitchell, *Multiple Staff Ministries* (Louisville: Westminster, 1988).

STRUCTURES OF HUMAN SYSTEMS
Concepts That Remind Leaders
of the Congregation as a Whole

These definitions are my own formulations of the concepts of many family systems theorists. This listing provides a quick reference of definitions of concepts illustrated in this chapter.

1. **Structures:** the way a system is ordered as seen in the arrangement, positioning, and relationships among the component parts of a system.

2. **Subsystems:** component organizational units that are established by **rules**, by **roles**, and by **rituals**. Roles, rules, and rituals may be formal or informal, explicit or tacit.

3. **Boundaries:** invisible, emotional borders to subsystems which limit access to relationships, information, and decision-making.

4. **Authority patterns:** accepted structures in which a person or group holds more or less limited authority over another person or group.

5. **Processes:** The ways members and groups interact with each other and change or stay the same within the structures. A human system maintains its balance by being more or less:

   a. **closed** (authoritarian, rule-bound, hierarchical, enmeshed, more concerned for the group than the individual),

   b. **open** (democratic, with shared decision-making and more flexible but orderly boundaries),

   c. or **random** (disengaged, with the individual valued over the group and less attention paid to rules and boundaries).

6. **Direction of Communication:**

   a. **Pursuing:** seeking emotional contact and/or physical closeness as a means of reducing anxiety; spontaneous, lively, emotionally responsive and talkative.

   b. **Distancing:** seeking emotional and/or physical distance as a means of reducing anxiety; reserved, calm, logical, and quiet.

   Pursuing and distancing are complementary roles in a human system. Two people need to be moving toward each other in order to communicate.

STRUCTURES OF HUMAN SYSTEMS (continued)
Concepts That Remind Leaders
of the Congregation as a Whole

7. **Responsibility Patterns**

   a. **Overfunctioning:** assuming responsibility for the actions, feelings, and well-being of others or of a group who are capable of being responsible for themselves. Sometimes defined as playing "savior."

   b. **Underfunctioning:** refraining from responsibility for one's own actions, feelings, and well-being, even though one is capable of being responsible for one's self. Sometimes defined as playing "victim."

   Overfunctioning and underfunctioning are complementary roles in a human system.

8. **Triangles:** three individuals or groups (or ideas or forces) who respond to each other in balanced or unbalanced ways, either rigid or flexible, based on the anxiety in the relationships.

   Generally observed rules of triangles are:

   Friend of my friend is my friend

   Friend of my enemy is my enemy

   Enemy of my friend is my enemy

   Enemy of my enemy is my friend

9. **Alliances and Coalitions:** Triangular relations often become unbalanced by coalitions.

   a. A **coalition** is two or more members of a system, often at different levels of authority (a member and a staff member, or a member and a member of a governing board), who join together expressly to oppose or exclude another person or group. A coalition usually involves secretiveness, and its existence is likely to be denied if someone asks about it.

   b. By contrast **an alliance** is two or more members of a system who agree to work together on an issue of common interest, without intentionally excluding or opposing others. An alliance is not usually secretive.

Observing Boundaries

As is the case in many congregations experiencing conflict, the boundaries around some of the subsystems at Big Bluff City were not very well defined. Boundaries are those invisible, emotional borders separating the subsystems from each other which define the relationships within them. The boundaries are not necessarily physical lines on a map, although we'll be mapping the structures of Big Bluff City Church in the next section. Rather they are social and emotional limits that define access to relationships. For example, by virtue of their regular meeting times members of the church board may have a special feeling of closeness with each other that other members of the congregation may not have. Access to decision-making is another boundary that was not very clearly defined in Big Bluff City Church. For example, some people were informally evaluating the job performance of the pastor and had decided the church needed to fire him. Formally, the authority to evaluate the pastor's performance and make recommendations regarding his continuation or dismissal was the domain of the personnel committee of the board. Access to information was an even more problematic boundary issue presented at Big Bluff City Church. Because members of opposing factions were able to find out who said what in a board meeting, it became nearly impossible for the board to have an honest and open discussion. Any discussion of a topic that was dear to the hearts of one of the factions was suppressed out of fear that their words would be repeated in anger by other members of the church or even by people in the community who were not members of the church.

Mapping Congregational Structures

One of the tools that Agnes and Bill used to examine the structures of Big Bluff City Church is called mapping. This approach is derived from the family systems practice of studying a family by drawing a genogram,[3] or a generational diagram, similar to a family tree,

---

3. For more information on the genogram see Becvar and Becvar, *Family Therapy,* 164–66. I have adapted the symbols from family systems theorists to apply to church situations. Compare with the chart in Becvar and Becvar, *Family Therapy,* 204.

SYMBOLS FOR MAPPING A CONGREGATION'S STRUCTURAL RELATIONSHIPS

A small circle indicates a particular woman.

A small square indicates a particular man.

Rectangles of various sizes represent formal structural entities such as a board, a committee, or other church body, placed so that the order of authority and subordination among the units is indicated.

Ovals of various sizes represent informal structures such as coalitions, alliances, or social groups.

Single lines indicate lines of accountability or connection.

Double darker lines indicate strong relationships.

Wavy lines indicate troubled or conflicted relationships.

Dotted lines indicate uncertain or unhealthy boundaries.

Dashed lines represent healthy boundaries around structures.

■ Roles of various members are printed next to their symbols (pastor, staff member, personnel chairperson, etc.).

■ Lines are drawn between individuals or groups indicating triangulation, with lines doubled or wavy to represent the conflicts or unbalanced nature of the triangles.

■ OF and UF next to individuals or groups indicate either overfunctioning or underfunctioning in the system.

Arrows indicate the direction of communication and the pursuing or distancing occurring in the system.

MAPPING BIG BLUFF CITY CHURCH

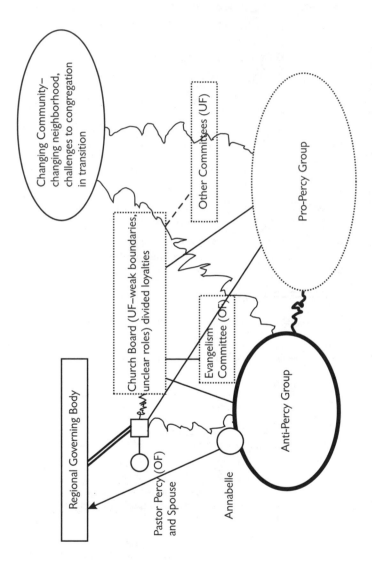

indicating the patterns of relationships among the members of the family. Mapping is a helpful way of creating a visual interpretation of a situation. Not only is it useful for people who learn best visually, it is also a good tool for people for whom words become inadequate for understanding what's happening. A map of a congregation depicts the various subsystems by a set of symbols with various kinds of lines (solid, dashed, dotted, etc.) indicating the patterns of relationship. It is eye-opening to see patterns emerge when mapping a group's behaviors.

Questions to Help You Look at Structures

Some of the early conversations that Agnes and Bill had with Percy and with the board at Big Bluff City were based on a series of questions designed by Kenneth Mitchell from his days at the Menninger Foundation. They selected a few of these questions to encourage the parties in the conflict to reflect on their situation as if they were anthropologists. Each question gets at a particular element of the structural architecture of a church or a group within a church. Mitchell provides sixteen questions, which include both structural issues and elements that are more suited to narrative or symptom assessment. For looking at structures, I have limited the questions to seven (see "Questions for Understanding Structures of a Congregation" on the following page). The first question under each number is the primary or theme question. Those that follow are designed to elicit more detail about each theme. Sometimes just doing this exercise produces insights and suggestions for change toward a healthier life together. At other times, a leader or consultant might need to ask more pointed questions about the relative health and vitality of the structures discovered in the exercise. Overall, the study questions help the members of the group see that they are engaged in an interconnected system that has its own life. The system will be seen as healthy or unhealthy, but it will be clear that the situations noted represent the group or church as a whole and not just particular members who have adopted unhealthy behaviors or attitudes.

QUESTIONS FOR UNDERSTANDING
STRUCTURES OF A CONGREGATION

1. What **subgroups** can you discern within the group you are studying, and what **supergroups** can you find of which this one is a
   member? What groups hold more or less authority over others?
   To what extent do conflict and cooperation exist among the
   groups you are studying? If you are studying a whole congregation, supergroups for the church would include the denomination
   and its regional body, as well as the community in which the
   congregation lives.

2. Describe the membership **boundaries,** that is, how does anyone
   know who is in and who is outside this group? Are the boundaries
   clear or unclear? Who are the gatekeepers of the boundaries?
   What specific information, relationships, and decisions are limited
   to members of your particular group?

3. Can you list no more than ten and no fewer than five **rules** that
   you believe are generally known and acknowledged throughout
   the group? Then list the same number of rules that you are relatively sure operate but the existence of which is generally not
   acknowledged or discussed in the group.

4. What **roles** are important in the operation of this group? Include
   formal, informal, and explicit and implicit roles. Are any important
   roles missing?

5. What **triangles** can you see in operation? Which triangles are
   based on unhealthy coalitions setting two people or groups against
   a third? Which triangles are healthier because they are flexible,
   shifting the alliances among the members on each corner of the
   triangle so that no two people are perpetually in coalition and no
   one person is perpetually excluded?

6. Can you list at least five **rituals** that define the character and
   maintain the relationships within the group you are studying? Are
   any of these rituals secretive — not generally known outside the
   group? What happens if someone fails to perform a ritual or if the
   performance is not carried out in accordance with the tradition of
   the group?

7. Are any of the formal and explicit structures **out of harmony**
   with the informal or implicit structures in the group? Are there
   any of these structures that appear to be out of harmony with the
   values of the group or its supergroup?

Adapted from Kenneth Mitchell, *Multiple Staff Ministries* (Louisville: Westminster
Press, 1988), 63–76.

Are the Structures Healthy?

Looking at structures helps a leader or participant or outside consultant to remember that the congregation is an interrelated whole. Often just remembering to think structurally can bring calm and a new perspective to the situation. A word of caution: structural family systems theory has been rightly criticized for imposing assumptions about what are healthy and unhealthy structures for client groups or families. Every congregation is unique and develops its own patterns of organization. Just as God created each living creature as its own gift, God has become incarnate in each congregation in creative and individual ways. There are no clear, externally defined rules for what is a healthy structure.

**CRITERIA FOR
HEALTHY STRUCTURES**

1. Subsystems serve their functions if their boundaries and roles and rules are honored so that decisions are made, information is known and shared, and relationships are maintained.

2. Information flows best in an open environment; secrets (as different from confidences) block the flow of appropriate and essential information.

3. A system needs a balance of individuality (difference) and community (resemblance) among its members and groups. Either closed process (too much community closeness, enmeshed) or random process (too much individuality and distance, disengaged) inhibits that healthy balance.

4. Structures need to adapt as the situation calls for it. Structures that are too rigid can be as unhelpful to the system as structures that are not strong enough.

But we can make general observations about the relative health of the particular structures in a particular congregation, drawn from the fields of family systems theory and systems theory in organizational management.

Applying these criteria to Big Bluff City Church we see that boundaries, particularly around the church board, were neither clear nor honored. As a program-sized church it needed roles to be consistent and boundaries to be flexible enough to adapt to the changing needs of the church and the community. The roles were poorly defined, and the pastor had overfunctioned by taking power that was not formally his. The pastor had also underfunctioned by not engaging in empowering leadership that encouraged the members of the church board to take their rightful roles. Much of the information flow at Big Bluff was in secret, along the lines of triangles. Coalitions talked to each other but not to their opponents. Differences were not respected or used for a rich discussion to discern what God was calling them to do or be. Annabelle took on a strong leadership role, going around the less healthy structures to call in the regional governing body for assistance. This was an appropriate call for help: even though her anxiety and her talkativeness made her appear to be a troublemaker, in fact she was acting on behalf of her congregation to call attention to the need for healthier ways to meet the challenges of their place and time.

Structural Hope
for Big Bluff City Church

If Agnes had done a simple diagnosis of the conflict at Big Bluff, it would have looked extremely hopeless. The pastor and a sizeable number of members were at an impasse, making angry accusations about each other and being unwilling to talk to each other. In many similar situations, the pastor is encouraged to leave, with or without a severance package to make the transition possible. In her role as the regional minister, Agnes was wise in the ways of congregations as interconnected systems and spent the extra time and effort to look at the structural realities in the congregation. The obvious over- and underfunctioning among the church leaders, from the pastor to the members of church committees, and the conspicuous disconnection between the formal rules and roles expected by their denomination for pastors and church leaders and the actual functioning of the pastor and the church board led the regional minister to try a structural intervention first.

Prompted by Annabelle's call for assistance and helped by a strong relationship between the pastor and the regional governing body, Agnes was able to arrange meetings with Percy, with the "anti-Percy" group, and finally with the church board. After two meetings of asking structural questions and observing the patterns of the board's interactions, Agnes and Bill recommended that two more meetings be scheduled to spend time studying the formal constitution of the congregation and its denomination. During the two study sessions, board members discovered resources they had never known before and became very enthusiastic about the authority inherent in their roles as lay leaders of the congregation. They decided very quickly to give up their passivity and become partners with their pastor in leading the congregation. They even recognized that they had enough authority to call to account any members of the congregation who were acting in destructive ways. Agnes and Bill gracefully withdrew from the situation, encouraging the new-found leadership to work diligently. However, they continued to coach Percy, helping him to remember his own sense of call to be the pastor to the congregation and encouraging him not to carry all the burdens of leadership. The conflict subsided fairly quickly after that, and the session went on to launch a major evangelism program to contact new residents in their neighborhood and invite them to worship. The church continues to be strong and healthy, thanks to some simple insights into the way God was calling the leaders to be healthier and more willing to face the changes in their community.

Reflection on
Looking at Structures

1. Identify some of the structural parts or subsystems in your congregation and name at least one rule, one role, and one ritual that defines each of those parts.

2. Think about the boundaries that establish and maintain relationships in the structural parts of your congregation. Are they rigid or flexible, chaotic or dependable?

3. Construct a map of the structures in your congregation and identify the boundaries that are healthy and those that are not so healthy. Note with straight or wavy lines where the relationships are strong and where they are conflicted. Let the map help you sort out the clues about the underlying realities that have contributed to the current conflict.

Chapter Four

Listening for Hope in Stories

Later on, without abandoning the concepts of family structure and family development, I began to focus on the particular story that a family constructs to make sense of their life. People have the habit of becoming the stories they tell. When memory speaks it tells a "narrative truth," which comes to have more influence than "historical truth." The "facts" presented to a therapist are partly historical truth and partly a construction. The constructs that become the shared reality of a family represent mutual understandings and shared prejudices, some of which are hopeful and helpful, some of which are not. — Salvador Minuchin[1]

Hope and Despair in Suburbia

The story of Endwell Community Church began with high hopes and great expectations. From the vantage point of six years of life together, members like to recount ways they remember God working to bring strangers together and making them friends. The committee of the Presbyterian regional governing body charged with birthing a new congregation looked at many different properties in the rapidly growing suburban area but could find nothing that fit their needs. However, just when the last piece of available vacant land slipped out of their hands, the denominational offices received a letter from another denomination announcing that a church building, within blocks of the demographic center of the target area, was for sale.

---

1. Salvador Minuchin, *Family Healing: Strategies for Hope and Understanding* (New York: Free Press, 1993), 43. See note 17 on page 21.

A large lot on a major highway with an existing church building seemed like a miracle. Within two years of occupying the new property, the members like to remember, they had grown to their present size of 150 members. Clearly God's hand was in it. The congregation adopted a blend of contemporary and traditional worship and organized themselves in the emerging fashion of a team-based mission structure.

A few years later these hopes had dimmed as the church went into a crisis of struggle and decline. Although the surrounding community was expected to continue to grow for another fifteen years, the rapid growth of the church's first two years slowed and stopped. Many factors could have played into the crisis. The population of the suburban area surrounding Endwell was mostly Methodist and Roman Catholic, leaving a small proportion to all the other denominations. Competition for the new congregation came from three of the largest Methodist congregations in the metropolitan area, which were located within five miles of Endwell, and at least five other new church developments in the same ministry area.

This sixth-year crisis was not the first they had experienced, of course. Several times in the short life of Endwell Church, when the budget was tight and leaders were discouraged, Lew, one of the lay leaders, had kept hopes high by summarizing their story: "God had something good in mind in founding this church, and although we can't see it now, that good is going to come about in due time. We've just got to hang in there until it does."

In that sixth year of their life together, however, the hopeful energy of the beginning years had turned to constant worries. The governing board deadlocked with unexpected and painful power struggles over recent proposals for new ministries and activities that were presented with the hope that they might move the church to attract more new members. Board members Kim and Ken had squared off against each other with anger and threats of withdrawal to force the board to go along with their personal opinions, one for and the other against the new programs, even when a large majority of the board would have voted in favor of the changes. These power struggles had eroded the lay leaders' energy for forward movement, and other members were entering the arguments about the future direction of the church. In response to these crises, Rob, the pastor who had begun the work of starting this church with great enthusiasm, suddenly lost all hope for the future of the church, and even worried about finding other work that could sustain him in the remaining years of his active ministry.

The church whose name suggested a full hope in God's ultimate care no matter what difficulties may be sustained had fallen into discouragement. An appreciation of the church's story, with its core narrative and a rhetorical assessment of its present difficulty, can help in the rediscovery of God's hand in the changes and chances of their present situation. Like the Israelites in exile in Babylon who put away their musical instruments because they could see no more reason to sing praises to God, the leaders and members at Endwell needed a new version of their story to pull them through the dark and despairing days.

Interpretation of Change and Hope

Since the conflict at Endwell was not extremely intense and several leaders were already attuned to the church's story, it was particularly well suited for listening to stories and assessing its narrative life. Nevertheless, emotions were high and many minds were confused by the complexity of the situation. In that context, leaders understandably forgot that they were called to be interpreters of a story rather than managers of conflict or controllers of the church's destiny. A simplistic mechanical assumption had taken over, in which diagnostic stop-action snapshots and X-rays were used to take the situation apart and find "the problem" which needed to be fixed.

This spirit of diagnosis was working against a loving and hopeful approach. By contrast, the spirit of interpretation would open the eyes and hearts of the leaders to the moving of God's Spirit in the situation. Change could begin to look more like a friend to be embraced than an enemy to be feared, and hope could return.

Narrative is woven deeply in the religious consciousness of every people around the globe. Many religious traditions interpret the stories of the people as the outcropping of the mind of the sacred. In the Judeo-Christian traditions particularly, God is often understood as Word. As a result the narrative life of a congregation may be seen as the interpretation of God's Word or story among them. The words or stories a congregation tells about itself are clues to its deeper realities and ultimately to the degree to which they are in harmony with the mind or will of God. As with the biblical stories, a congregation can learn to listen to the "metaphor, hyperbole, and ambiguity — to which could be added irony, incongruity, and contradiction"[2] of their own stories to see how God is influencing the drama of their lives. This allows us to see God and God's people as actors, agents in an unfolding drama of life in the world. Listening to and interpreting the stories of Endwell Church can give leaders a way to move beyond blaming and worrying to the new possibilities in their future.

Gathering Stories

The narrative approach[3] to church conflict is more collaborative than looking at structures and learning from symptoms. When the members and leaders are open to conversation, one or two leaders can become collectors of stories, like folklorists visiting another culture to sample their unique way of communicating. If one begins with the assumption that the congregation conveys its sense of identity in narrative form, listening to stories is an entryway into the inner wisdom of a congregation.

---

2. Walter Brueggemann, *Theology of the Old Testament* (Minneapolis: Fortress Press, 1997), 111.

3. I continue to follow Minuchin's focus on story as the family reality, but my approach is informed by other narrative theory, including that of James Hopewell, *Congregation: Stories and Structures* (Minneapolis: Fortress, 1987), and the narrative therapy movement, which has a close affinity to family therapy. I appreciate the narrative approach that makes the therapist a sort of co-dramatist with the family, but I want to hold on to Minuchin's more activist model of the therapist as I envision the leader interacting with the narratives of a congregation. See Minuchin's article "Where Is the Family in Narrative Family Therapy?" *Journal of Marital and Family Therapy* 24, no. 4 (1998): 397–418.

Careful Listening

The first way to gather stories is simply to observe the interactions of the congregation itself. To paraphrase Yogi Berra, "You can hear a lot just by listening." Clues about the congregation's story can be found by paying attention to what the congregation calls itself, the building in which they meet, and the rituals they practice. For example, here's what that would have looked like in the case of Endwell Church.

Name. The name of each church contains its own little story. Endwell was the name of a small town founded in the nineteenth century, which had been transformed into a sprawling suburb in the last decade of the twentieth century. The name was literally taken from the title of a Shakespeare comedy, *All's Well That Ends Well.* In the last quarter of the twentieth century the city leaders, seeing the trends of population growth, changed the name to "Northgate" to convey something more contemporary. By selecting the older name the new congregation chose to hold on to both the older identity of the community and the comic perspective that, no matter how bad it looks now, it all will turn out well in the end.

Building. The preexisting building of the Endwell Church carried its own story, which may or may not influence the story of the present congregation. The previous congregation of another denomination had experienced a crisis over a doctrinal controversy, and half of the congregation formed another congregation in a neighboring suburb. The remaining group was unable to continue to function as a church. The building reverted back to the parent denomination, which placed it on the market. While the location of the building was good for church growth, listening to the stories belonging to the building can give some insight into the current crisis for the Endwell Church. Some of the stories of the previous congregation served as lessons for the leaders at Endwell in their efforts to prevent their congregation from becoming insular and dying for lack of attention to their mission to the community. Nevertheless, the residents of the neighborhood continued to have a hard time imagining that anything good would come of a church in that building because of its history.

Rituals and Music. Little habits and artifacts in a congregation's life often capture the personality and perspective of that group of people. The repetition of a particular prayer, moving about the worship space at the pastor's direction to greet each other, or the presence of a particular work of art can convey a sense of who these people are together. A part of the story for Endwell Church is contained in the "theme song" informally adopted by the congregation. The hymn "The Lone, Wild Bird" was the most sung and most requested of the whole hymn book over the past six years. It has a lovely, lilting melody and is easy to sing, but the image of a tiny bird flying through the skies in full view of God conveys something of the loneliness of suburban living and reassures the singer that even in solitary flight to unknown places, God's spirit is present. Perhaps this song also became a favorite because the opening words of the second stanza as written by Henry Richard McFayden echo the name of the Endwell congregation: "The ends of the earth are in your hand."[4] The music director even found two more verses based on the sections of Psalm 139 about God's care for each one from before birth to now, and about God's searching, knowing love, connecting the song to the deep sense of prayer in the life of this particular congregation. The song gives some clues to the overall story of the congregation.

Collaborative Collection of Stories

To gather information about stories, a leader is wise to use regular gatherings, classes, or special meetings to encourage reflection on the church's story. In preparation for these gatherings, members are invited to bring pictures, clippings, worship bulletins, newsletters, keepsakes, or other memorabilia that will help tell the story of their congregation. When people are together the story collector can ask them to get into small groups and begin to tell each other the stories that the artifacts suggest. Creating a historical timeline on which to attach these artifacts can be a way of inviting even more memories.

---

4. Lyrics copyright 1927 by *The Homiletic and Pastoral Review*.

People can review their stories by reflecting on what the stories tell them about what they want to remember about the church as a family, about the vision and purpose of the church, about being part of a particular denomination, about traditions that hold them together, about what makes worship important in their congregation, and about the spiritual and moral landmarks of their lives together.

Drawing on a few of these stories, which of course reflect only a sample of the richness of the narrative life of a congregation, leaders can encourage at least three ways of drawing the meanings from the congregation's stories — narrative interpretation, story typing, and appreciative inquiry.

Interpreting Narrative Patterns

Interpreting a congregation's stories is like studying literature. It entails identifying and interpreting the patterns of repeating themes, naming the chief characters of the stories and the roles they play in the drama, noting the voices that are not heard, and examining the plotting of the story as it links, twists, turns, and thickens. Unlike the literature study sometimes taught in high school, however, no authority can tell us the right interpretation of the patterns we discover. Only the congregation members themselves can decide what the patterns identified in studying their stories mean to them.

Repeating Themes

The stories folks told at Endwell Church contained several themes that kept repeating themselves.

- There was great energy and enthusiasm for participation in the life of the church. The early meetings held, even during snowstorms, to identify the mission and activities of the church were heavily attended. A group of volunteers gathered on Saturday mornings to refurbish the church sanctuary, moving cabinets, rearranging chairs, placing banners, and arranging the sound system.

- Friendship and fellowship kept coming up in conversations. Pot luck dinners, parties, celebrations of holy seasons, the inclusion of a Vietnamese immigrant family in the life of the congregation were the common experience of a group of people who had not known each other prior to the founding of Endwell Church.

- The children of the congregation were celebrated and coddled in special ways. The kids told their own stories about the church, and many had their own nicknames for the church.

- Struggles figured heavily in the stories. The campaign to pay off the mortgage on the building so that new growth could happen was a strong memory. A struggle for attention and support from the denominational offices was another repeating story.

- Prayer was a key theme. More than half the people present told about being helped through illnesses or painful difficulties after asking the congregation for prayer.

- A discord could be noted as Pastor Rob's stories compared and contrasted the other repeating themes. Rob told a "future story" of a congregation of four hundred members, with strong youth and children's programs, a vital worship experience, and service to the community. Neither pastor nor lay leaders seemed to recognize that the emphasis on close relationships and deep connections in many of the themes were in disharmony with the pastor's hope for a larger, more complex congregation. The idea of a larger congregation was threatening to those who liked the simplicity of the relationships in a church of 125 in worship.

Characters in the Stories

Every congregational story has characters who are unique, significant, and memorable. As we get acquainted with a story, we begin to care about what happens to each of the characters as they interact and move the story along. As the story of Endwell Church has been recounted so far, four names have been mentioned — Pastor Rob, Lew, the elder who held out the hopeful, comic view, and Kim and Ken, the battling elders. Reflecting on the narrative roles that key characters play helps to put into a larger, more systemic perspective the emotional toll their interactions are exacting. "Characters in Church Narratives" on the following page lists the types of roles people play in conflicted systems.

Ken began the most recent chapter of the church's story as a leader, heading a mission committee that had studied the needs of the community and the resources of the church and was proposing an exciting and challenging program of service to the children of the community. The program would entail some physical changes to the building and would involve expenses not currently in the budget. Ken had even received commitments from individual church members to contribute the extra money needed to start this ministry. When the proposal came to the church board for final action, Kim rose up in fierce opposition, making unfair accusations against Ken and his committee and threatening to resign if the board approved the plan. At that point, Kim appeared to be a villain, oppositional and destructive. Because Kim and Ken were employed by competing companies in the area, their clash took on personal overtones, and Ken quickly became a reactor and a victim, in turn threatening to withdraw his own money and his commitment to the congregation. The other members of the church board, who had been ready to vote to approve the plan, assumed victim roles themselves as they dithered about the personal nature of the clash between Kim and Ken and were unable either to make decisions or to find a way to mediate the conflict. Also falling out of character as leader was Pastor Rob, who interpreted Kim's surprise opposition and Ken's uncharacteristic tantrum as acts of sabotage to the forward movement of the congregation and further evidence for his own sense of victimization.

A narrative interpretation might have helped the leaders of Endwell Church to see the truth and potential for transformation in this episode of conflict. If someone had listened to Kim long enough, they might have identified her role as a homeostat for the congregation instead of a villain. She recognized that the new program had the potential to change the nature of the congregation, and she feared the loss of closeness and attention to prayer and fellowship

CHARACTERS IN CHURCH NARRATIVES

Leader: one who acts from an inner sense of freedom and integrity and an outer demeanor of respectful communion with others to move the congregation's story into the future (see chapter 8).

Hero-Savior: one who seeks relief from anxiety by controlling or overfunctioning for the sake of the congregation, relieving others of their responsibility to lead with their own inner wisdom and gifts.

Victim: one who seeks relief from anxiety by underfunctioning, refraining from appropriate leadership, sometimes blaming others for failures or suffering. Sometimes victims think of themselves as heroes, too.

Identified Problem Person: sometimes known as the symptom bearer or scapegoat, one who is either universally blamed for the problems of the rest of the church or whose personal problems deflect the attention of the church from other issues of change or interrelated anxieties.

Helper: one who moves the story forward by encouraging others to take appropriate leadership roles, sometimes a catalyst for action.

Reactor: one who moves the story forward by emotional reaction to the actions of others inside or outside the system. The reactor could work on fusion by insisting on closeness and sameness, or on fission by splitting the congregation or withdrawing from the system.

Homeostat: one who is sensitive to changes and who works to bring the system back into emotional balance, usually by insisting that deviations from the status quo change back.

Villain: one who acts in hurtful or destructive ways to become an enemy of a leader or hero.

that met her own needs at Endwell. Some helper in the situation might have noted that the mission plan indeed had a somewhat threatening aspect because it represented the possible losses that all change brings with it. Reflection on the narrative characters might have been enough to encourage more leadership and helping and less reaction and helplessness.

Unheard Voices

A narrative approach might also have helped Kim to acknowledge that she thought of herself as representing the unheard voices of members of the congregation who were not leaders. She intuitively recognized a minority of folks who did not want the small-church nature of Endwell Church to change. Ken, Pastor Rob, and elder Lew based their actions on a story line that imagined the church continuing to grow beyond its single-cell stage into a program-sized church with an identity of community service. That story was out of harmony with the other stories that celebrated the importance of fellowship, food, and personal relationships with all the members of the congregation. In one sense, the conflict was larger than the personal rift between Ken and Kim. They also represented competing stories about the church's future and the role of change in the life of the congregation. Asking about unheard voices can encourage members and leaders to enrich and enhance the story by bringing the dissonant voices and stories together in a richer, more interesting, and more truthful narrative.

Interpreting Story Types

A simple and quick way into understanding church stories is through methods of interpretation taken from both biblical and literary studies.[5] Four types of church story can be found by listening and asking questions:

---

5. Marcus Borg, *Meeting Jesus Again for the First Time* (New York: Harper-Collins, 1994).

The Exodus: A Romantic Story

Romantic stories have heroes and heroines who strive against titanic forces. The battles are always terrible, and in most romances the heroes tend to be in danger of failure until divine intervention turns the story from failure to success. Moses is the great hero of the People of God who returns to Egypt to free a nation of slaves. But the power of the Egyptian empire is too great for him. Too great, that is, until God intervenes and overwhelms the Egyptian Pharaoh and changes his mind. In fact another divine intervention is required before the escaping people can cross the sea to safety. The Gospels portray Jesus as the savior whose very life represents the intervention of God into human life for transformation and salvation.

The Exile: A Comic Story

Comedies are not necessarily funny. By formal definition, a story is comical when the hero fails to see reality and gets mired in mistaken expectations, but is enlightened in the end and made to see what is really going on. A comedy has a "happy ending" when the characters are able to see that what they thought was a terrible situation is not so bad after all. When God's people are separated from home and temple and God, they tend to believe that all is lost. However, as Isaiah told the exiles, "God's ways are not your ways." Once they are able to see how God is working in their situation, they will be able to return home and center their lives on God. In the Gospels, Jesus is portrayed as the teacher who is able to show people the true nature of life in God, to open their eyes to God's goodness and love, and in this sense Jesus is a comic type.

The Priestly Drama of the Temple: Tragic Stories

In classic tragedies, the heroes are pitted against the unalterable laws of God, and nothing they can do can make them perfect enough. They are separated from God by their tragic flaws or their sinfulness. The absolute justice of God demands that sin be punished by death. The drama of the temple in the Hebrew scriptures is a substitution of an unblemished animal, placed as an offering on the altar,

---

FOUR QUESTIONS TO HELP YOU INTERPRET YOUR CONGREGATION'S STORY TYPES

Ask a representative group of people to read the following four statements and indicate which story type appeals most to them.

1. Humans are victims, in bondage to social and spiritual life-destroying forces, and as in the Exodus, God intervenes in Jesus Christ to overcome those forces and make us free.

2. Humans are lost, lonely, and longing for a spiritual home, and as in the Exile, God shows us, through Jesus Christ, the way home to God.

3. Humans are sinners, guilty in the sight of God, and as in the priestly drama of the Temple, Jesus Christ died to forgive our sins.

4. Humans experience both joy and suffering in a life that seems absurd, and as in the wisdom literature, God stands with us as a mysterious presence in Jesus Christ.

Tally and compare the number of responses to each question. A congregation usually has a dominant type of story characterization and a secondary type, which is close or complementary to it.

---

in place of the sinful human being. Following this story, Jesus was interpreted as the "sacrificial lamb" whose death satisfied the just law of God and thus saved believers from death.

Wisdom Literature: Ironic Stories

The fourth story type is the Ironic Story. The characters in ironic stories are not so much heroes and heroines as ordinary people, plugging along trying to make sense out of their lives. Life has its ups and downs, its joys and its sufferings, and the primary meaning that can be found is in caring for each other. The ironic strain in the Bible is found mainly in the wisdom literature. Job is the best known ironic character in the Bible; he faced terrible suffering and found no answer except the absolute mystery of God. The Gospels have a wisdom theme running through them in which Jesus is interpreted as the Word of God and a teacher of the wisdom of God. Jesus experienced the joys and sufferings of human life and remained faithful to the mysterious presence of God through them all.

A clue to the story type for Endwell Church was in the words of the elder who advised the other leaders to hold on until God can make something good happen here. That is a classic comic perspective: "We may feel lost and hopeless, but that's just because we're in the middle of this story. It will unfold into something beautiful if we stay faithful to the God who brought us together." When the pastor administered the story type questions to the congregation one Sunday morning, it was clear that the majority were evenly split between the comic and the ironic viewpoints. A smaller group of members identified themselves with the tragic type, and they were characteristically those who opposed many of the new styles of church life practiced there. One interpretation of the era of discouragement would be to see a conflict between the more conventional ironists and the more experimental comedists. Instead of being patient with each other and with God, the ironists were insisting on the importance of solidarity with all the members against those who wanted to try more new outreach programs to bring in newer members. The pastor's discouragement, in fact, may have been due to his own deep sense of ironic freedom in which God is more or less absent from the direction of the church and it is up to the leaders and members to make it what it can become. A touch more comedy might have eased his heart and mind.

Interpretation with Appreciative Inquiry

Another way to gather stories to make sense of the congregation as an interconnected whole is through appreciative inquiry. Sharing theoretical roots with family systems theory, appreciative inquiry has been a fruitful addition to the work of conflict utilization.[6] At Endwell Church, the process was used with the church board to empower and energize that group to interpret the present crisis as hopeful rather than discouraging. At the invitation of the pastor and with the approval of the board Dr. Marshall, a local university professor, spent three sessions with the board encouraging them to tell their stories and the church's stories in a positive, hopeful fashion.

A Congregation-Wide Process

In the first meeting, Dr. Marshall described the process of appreciative inquiry (AI) as a way of listening to stories. He encouraged the group to set aside their "problem solving" mind-sets and focus for a while on the strengths and health at Endwell Church. "Let's tell each other stories of joy and blessing, of times when people were faithful, when challenges were met, and when programs were effective," he said as he wrote questions on the whiteboard on the wall of the meeting room. The questions were:

1. Remembering your entire experience at Endwell Church, when were you most alive, most motivated, and most excited about your involvement? What made it exciting? Who else was involved? What happened? What was your part? Describe what you felt.

2. What do you value most about the church? What activities or ingredients or ways of life are most important? What are the best features of the church?

3. What three wishes would you make for the future of the church?[7]

He then invited the elders to divide into teams of two and spend about forty-five minutes asking each other the questions and listening carefully for the stories, taking notes as they went along.

---

6. Mark Branson, *Memories, Hopes and Conversations: Appreciative Inquiry and Congregational Change* (Herndon, VA: Alban Institute, 2004).
7. Ibid., 7.

As the pairs shared their stories the energy in the room was amazing. A group that was struggling to keep their morale up was suddenly finding more good than they had imagined in their church. As an example, Frannie was telling her partner of one of the first controversies in the church. Pastor Rob had introduced the inclusive language "Doxology" in worship at the very beginning, but in the first year, as members began taking more responsibility for the worship service, a disagreement arose about whether to continue to use that version or return to the more traditional "Praise Him all Creatures. . . . " Frannie remembers the meeting at which the shy mother of a young child spoke up to say that she liked the "old" version better, but that her daughter had memorized the "new" one and she would not want to change it back for her daughter's sake. That mother's testimony carried the meeting to keep the more inclusive version. This was a story of how the Endwell Church had made decisions about controversial subjects based on the needs of the future generation and not just on the preferences of the present leadership. The group recognized that Frannie's story could help make sense of the present conflict. Other stories of health and joy were shared around the room that evening. In response to their experience with the initial questions, Dr. Marshall described the assumptions behind AI to the group, including its emphasis on what works well, its attention to the impact of the focus of inquiry, the importance of continuity in moving into the future, and the way appreciative inquiry uses energy and collaboration to move a congregation forward into the future.[8]

At the next meeting, Dr. Marshall described the process for further gathering of stories and for turning them into hopeful plans for the future. The church board enthusiastically appointed a task force of three of its members and two other members of the church to be a listening team to engage a larger part of the congregation in the questions and conversations of appreciative inquiry. The group agreed that the focus of the work would be positive and that the questions would seek stories of life-giving resources available to the

---

8. Ibid., 24.

congregation. With Dr. Marshall's help, the leaders had embarked on a process of listening to the stories of Endwell Church.

Drawing Out the Themes

The second step in appreciative inquiry is to gather the stories together and collaboratively draw out the themes that appear in the stories. Themes are the common elements of story that indicate that a church is not a collection of individuals but rather an organic whole.[9] Interpreters listen for high energy behind repeating events — where people report some sense of excitement, accomplishment, or purpose — which suggests the themes can draw individuals and groups into action.[10] The stories gathered by the listening team at Endwell pointed to themes like the following:

* A sense of joy and surprise that people found themselves in a church that both provided friendship and challenged their notions about what church could be. ("I did not think I'd like the contemporary music, but it's a lot more fun than the stodgy old hymns we used to sing.")

* A genuine ownership in the church, not depending on the pastor and other leaders to do all the work; rather, each member's voice made a difference (memories of the "open forum" meetings held periodically to set the direction and structure of the church).

* An identity derived from the "minority" status of Presbyterians among the Catholics and Methodists. ("It's a good place to be myself instead of what all my neighbors think religion is supposed to be.")

* A pride in the ability of the church to face its problems and its limitations and make something good happen from the problem.

* The ability of the leaders and congregation to adapt to the developmental needs of a young church. For example, one member

---

9. Hopewell, *Congregation*, 194–95.

10. Branson, *Memories, Hopes and Conversations*, 80, and Thomas Groome, *Sharing Faith: A Comprehensive Approach to Religious Education and Pastoral Ministry, the Way of Shared Praxis* (San Francisco: HarperSanFrancisco, 1991), 156.

reported: "I'm impressed with the way the pastor shifted from his initial role as director of the newly started congregation to collaborative leader with the other leaders who had emerged in the early phases of the church's life."

The energy initially felt by the church board in answering the general questions continued to build in the listening team as they played with the themes that arose. The process of appreciative inquiry has the advantage of beginning to move a congregation toward more health in the early stages of gathering information. In chapter 7, we'll pick up the narrative themes, particularly the methods and processes of appreciative inquiry, and discuss ways to challenge the stories to move into a collective imagining of stories of the future.

Finding Hope in Stories of Conflict

A congregation in conflict is likely to be bound to the present with the emotion and anxiety that a conflict can evoke. The participants in the fight become focused on the present dilemma and on the shock and pain of the immediate past — who did what, who said what. Discouragement and despair are natural companions to a sense of stuckness in the present. When parties to the conflict cannot imagine a way out of the situation, or when they fear that the life of their congregation may come to an end, they have lost hope. Pastoral counselors have learned to listen to and interpret the stories their clients tell about the future and determine whether the stories help people move into the future with energy and commitment, or whether the stories inhibit action that would lead to healthier, happier tomorrows.[11]

The Endwell congregation had gotten stuck in the present. The church board and the pastor had lost their perspective on the story by assuming there was nothing they could do to make the future any brighter. No doubt the pastor was tired, perhaps weary of his role as savior-hero for the church. Dr. Marshall encouraged them to think

11. Andrew Lester, *Hope in Pastoral Care and Counseling* (Louisville: Westminster John Knox Press, 1995).

about their situation as an ongoing story line. The present situation could be interpreted as an unexpected twisting or thickening of the plot. The story continues to unfold with the members and leaders waiting, like interested readers, to see what will happen next. In fact, as characters in the story, they had choices to make and their own actions would shape the next scenes and chapters of their church's life. Remembering that their church's name had a comic dimension, they realized that while they did not see what was in their future, they could trust that the story would turn out all right in the end.

With Dr. Marshall's help, Pastor Rob acknowledged both his weariness and his need to change his role from savior back to leader. In his reflection and discernment, he decided his best leadership would be to leave. Within a year he had accepted a call to another church. In his farewell sermon, Rob used the text "For we know that all things work together for good for those who love God." And then he recited Salman Rushdie's "Haroun and the Sea of Stories."[12] With the additional twist of Rob's departure and the narrative coaching of Dr. Marshall, the congregation did drink from the sea of stories and was refreshed.

Through narrative interpretation, Kim was able to recognize her constructive role as a listener to unheard voices. She was able to relinquish her role as the homeostatic barrier to change as long as the other voices were heard and woven into the fabric of the story. In response to the twists and thickening of their story-line, the congregation regained its sense of the comic, and the board reconsidered and approved the ministry project. The little congregation moved into the next chapter of its life with hope and courage and a deep sense of gratitude that when the story gets dark and discouraging, the faithful stand true and firm, taking action as leaders and helpers, to work toward God's good ends. From time to time, they refreshed themselves with the story Pastor Rob told as he left them.

Haroun was a young boy whose mother left the home and whose father in despair lost his gift for storytelling. In response, Haroun

---

12. Salman Rushdie, *Haroun and the Sea of Stories* (New York: Penguin Books, 1990), 71–72.

went on an adventure in which he met a spiritual guide named Iff, the Water Genie. In this story about stories, the magical Water Genie conjured up for the discouraged Haroun "the Ocean of the Streams of Story." Before Haroun's eyes a stunning vision of "a thousand thousand thousand and one different currents, each one a different colour," twisted and turned in a marvelous display. "These are the Streams of Story," explained Iff the Water Genie. "Each coloured strand contains a single saga. Each part of the ocean holds its own kinds of stories. In fact, all of the stories that have ever been told and many that are still in the process of being invented are flowing here in this Ocean!" As he looked, Haroun realized that the stories were all in fluid form and had the ability to change and grow and interact with other stories to become newer stories yet untold. This was no storehouse of stories. It was alive. Then Iff the Water Genie, with a flourish, pulled a little golden cup from his costume, artfully dipped the cup into one of the streams of the Ocean, and offered it to Haroun with these words: "Let the magic of story restore your spirits! Guaranteed to make you feel A-Number One!" And Haroun accepted the cup, drank, and was very much refreshed.

Reflection on
Listening to Stories

1. Spend some quiet time to consider the extent to which you are engaging in diagnosis of your church's situation. Invite yourself to shift your heart and mind into the role of interpreter of the congregation's stories.

2. Identify how the name of your church, its mission statement, key beliefs, and common words, phrases, and songs might be interpreted as clues to the reality beneath the conflict in your congregation.

3. Name several of the key players in the current conflict situation and take on the role of story interpreter by identifying the narrative character each one is playing.

4. Engage in an anthropological study of your congregation by asking questions of other members about the types of stories they tend to identify with in order to help interpret its worldview.

5. Explore with other leaders the possibility of doing an appreciative inquiry into the narrative life of your congregation.

6. As you consider your congregation's stories, notice where hope is present or absent.

Chapter Five

Learning from Symptoms

When families come to me for help, I assume they have prob-
lems not because there is something inherently wrong with
them but because they've gotten stuck — stuck with a struc-
ture whose time has passed, and stuck with a story that doesn't
work. To discover what's bogging them down, I look for
patterns to connect.   — Salvador Minuchin[1]

When Everything the Leader Does to Help Makes It Worse

The personnel committee of the Old Hickory Church told interim
pastor Walt Lindsey that their main problem was their staff. During
the tenure of their former head of staff, Jason, there were constant
conflicts centered on Jill and Don, who were married to each other
and who served as the Christian education director and the music
director respectively. Jill and Don had managed to create roles for
themselves that were equal to Jason's. They had arranged, for example, to design the entire worship service each Sunday, including
selection of music and hymns, without reference to the sermon topic
chosen by the pastor. Further, they staffed their worship and Christian education committees as independent agencies not accountable
to the church board. Of course these conflicts carried over to the
congregation, with some members complaining about the style of
worship that had evolved under their leadership and others being
fully supportive of Jill and Don. The personnel committee had also

---

1. Salvador Minuchin, *Family Healing: Strategies for Hope and Understanding*
(New York: Free Press, 1993), 43.

intervened frequently in conflicts between other staff members and Jill and Don.

So at the beginning of his interim contract with the church, Walt was asked by the personnel committee to restore a more traditional authority pattern and to take charge of the worship services. Walt planned a simple structural intervention of reviewing all the roles and rules of the staff relationship and recommending the redistribution of the workload among the staff, including himself and Jill and Don. At the first staff retreat, however, this suggestion was met with extreme disappointment from Don and Jill, who nevertheless acquiesced to the new arrangements. Besides difficulties with the staff, Walt subsequently discovered that the church board had functioned as a rubber stamp to the staff recommendations, so he set into motion structural studies to empower the board members to take more leadership in their congregation. This further upset Jill and Don, who were used to a totally staff-run church organization. Staff meetings often were punctuated with angry words or silent tears.

Walt's relationship with Don and Jill was not always difficult, however, because they also began to share helpful stories about the congregation's life and history. That's how he learned of a public secret in the history of the congregation. Two pastors ago, prior to Jason, Rev. Morton had resigned without warning and had become a pastoral counselor, claiming burnout in his role as pastor. However, several of Jill and Don's sources indicated that Morton had been engaged in a sexual relationship with a former member who moved away to take a job in another city. No one in the congregation talked openly about these indiscretions, however, and Rev. Morton was still involved in the life of the congregation. As that story unfolded Walt began to hear tales of pastors before Morton who had also crossed sexual boundaries with church members and staff members. The stories went back as far as fifty years. In response to these themes, Walt made several efforts in informal groups and in sermons on the topic to begin conversations about the boundaries of professional staff. Neither the church board nor church members were willing to talk about such matters.

**WHEN TO MOVE FROM
STRUCTURES AND STORIES TO SYMPTOMS**

◆ When the system is cloudy or confused.

◆ When members of the system resist open conversation.

◆ When simple structural or narrative interventions make no
difference or make the conflict more intense.

When Walt came down with a serious bronchial infection in mid-winter, he recognized that his best efforts were not working. His own symptoms finally got his attention. A more difficult learning process was going to be required for his leadership at Old Hickory. Simple structural and narrative correctives were not going to work. He began to look more carefully at the symptoms and at the deeper issues to which they pointed.

First Lessons on Symptoms — Noticing Change

Learning is not an easy thing for us as church leaders. In itself, it requires change. It involves a disruption of one's area of comfort and expertise. Walt was beginning to recognize that he was going to have to do some real homework to help his congregation find hope.

Of course he was aware that Old Hickory Church had a long and venerable history dating back to the earliest days of European settlement in the area. In the previous twenty years the church had grown from a small congregation to a nearly corporate-sized church. For example, the current sanctuary had been a compromise to keep up with the growth process twenty years earlier, but limitations in its design made it less than appealing to most members of the congregation now. Walt also remembered his conversation with Pastor Jason a few months earlier. As Jason had attempted to consolidate the changes he perceived into the life of the church, he had

---

PRECURSORS TO CONFLICT
THAT CALL ATTENTION TO SYMPTOMS

Leaders can anticipate conflict as a response of the congregation as an interrelated whole, and can look back after conflict has erupted to see the precursors and to consider symptoms as signs change.

1. Changes in the family of the spiritual leaders, either clergy or lay, such as a birth, death, illness, divorce, change of address, marital problems or acting out of a child, or problems in the extended family of the pastor or the pastor's spouse.

2. Changes in the professional life of the clergy or lay leaders such as personal advancement, achievement of a degree, involvement in a civic project.

3. Changes in the long-term constituency of the parish, or the size of the congregation.

4. Changes in the staff of the congregation, such as the hiring, firing, or resignation of key staff members.

Source: Edwin Friedman, *Generation to Generation* (New York: Guilford, 1985), 203–4.

---

run into difficulty not only with his ministerial colleagues, but also with particular groups in the congregation. In the two years prior to Jason's departure, in fact, the membership had begun a slow and barely discernible decline. These reflections revealed that the church that Walt Lindsey had inherited for his interim service was in full-scale transition once again. In fact, when Walt began to reflect on the course of changes in the life of the church, he began to relax and be more confident about the possibility of his helping that church move through the transition into a healthier chapter in its life.

Old Hickory Church had just experienced the loss of their beloved pastor, Jason, and they were beginning to see the changes in the size and make-up of the congregation. In fact, the long-term constituency changes had been part of the transformation of that congregation for more than twenty years. In addition, the personnel committee had noted that things started getting more intense in the staff at Old Hickory when Jason had received his pastoral counseling certification and licensure. With that many changes in its recent history we should not be surprised at the presence of conflict at Old Hickory.

What Is a "Symptom"?

Because we do not commonly think of problems presented to us as symptoms, I want to discuss this concept a little more here. By usual definition, a symptom is the sign of something else. We have grown so used to medical terminology that uses the term to refer to a disease or disorder that we have forgotten its original sense of being a signal or sign. A sign is not the thing itself; it merely points to or represents the other thing. That which is pointed to is either not physically present or is not readily perceived by the senses. The stop sign calls attention to the social custom and law that require an orderly procession of traffic through an intersection; it does not in itself forcibly stop approaching cars. A red octagon does not, in itself, halt a car. It signals a larger systemic need for order. In the field of mental health, symptoms are always seen as indicators of internal difficulty or conflict, and they have the added quality of being "beyond one's control."[2] As we apply these ideas to a congregation, I hope you can begin to see that the problems that present themselves in a crisis are not necessarily intentional on the part of any person or group. Instead they are more likely to be the equivalent of the symptoms of pain, swelling, rise in temperature, rapid heartbeat, or high blood pressure in the individual human body. Since the turbulence in a congregation is not chosen or intended, leaders

---

2. Dorothy Stroh Becvar and Raphael J. Becvar, *Family Therapy: A Systemic Integration* (Boston: Allyn and Bacon, 2000), 241.

are called to careful observation and imaginative learning to determine what the troubles or symptoms are signaling about the life of a congregation.

I believe that conflict arises from the strain of inner or outer forces of change in the life of a congregation. In keeping with the emphasis on health, the first task of a leader is to find the way the difficulty or symptom serves the health and well-being of the congregation. Just as individuals with the best of intentions sometimes choose unhelpful solutions to their problems, so too do congregations. Learning from symptoms means shifting our viewpoint. The behaviors of conflict that we first viewed as problematic can be understood differently. Problematic actions of church members usually arise out of the anxiety of change in order to protect the identity of the church, or serve to protect the perceived power base of a particular group or individual. These actions can also be viewed as symptoms of something else going on, pointing to the good future that God desires for the congregation.

Learning from Symptoms at Old Hickory

For leaders, learning from symptoms is a more arduous exercise than looking at structures and listening to stories. It requires a more exacting mental attitude because it goes against the conventional wisdom of church life. Our usual intuition is to seek the "cause" of the problem, which usually means finding a single source of the difficulty and attempting to neutralize it or eliminate it. I have discovered that it's better to look more deeply to learn how the conflict points to a congregation's responses to changes in its life. Learning from symptoms requires the leader to see not only the wider difficulties in the church, but also how the leader is implicated in the situation itself.

While the ways that churches express their discomfort with changes are nearly infinite, we can identify a list of common types of symptoms (see the box on the following page). In our case study, the interim pastor was able to identify and begin to interpret all four types of symptoms in the Old Hickory Church situation. It

---

**COMMON SYMPTOMS
IN CONGREGATIONAL CONFLICT:
Patterns of Behavior Identified as a "Problem"
That Point to Changes in a Congregation
as an Interrelated Whole**

1. Expression of emotion or presence of pain that is out of proportion to the issues involved.

2. Noticeable or significant over- and underfunctioning.

3. Blaming one person or group for many of the church's problems; projecting the system's turmoil on an identified problem person.

4. Physical or emotional impairment in key leaders.

Source: Ronald Richardson, *Creating a Healthier Church* (Minneapolis: Fortress, 1996), 131–40.

---

was a relief for him to begin to distinguish between his own emotions and reactions and the reactions of the congregation. Learning to distinguish these sets of behavior as symptoms helped him refresh his efforts to provide leadership to the congregation to help them address their underlying struggle for health and transformation.

Here are some of the symptoms that Interim Pastor Walt identified at Old Hickory.

1. Expression of emotion or presence of pain that is out of proportion to the issues involved.

As Walt Lindsey reflected on possible symptoms in the Old Hickory situation, he remembered that Jill resorted to either tears or angry attacks on Walt whenever she felt he was "directing" her work, or as changes in the life of the church were proposed. Without taking away her right to express emotion in a working team, Walt noted that her reactions were more intense than the issues deserved. These behaviors looked like symptoms of some other patterns of difficulty.

2. Noticeable or significant over- and underfunctioning.

The staff at Old Hickory were overfunctioners, assuming heroic responsibility for the program and ministry and care of the entire congregation. The culture was one of overwork, and the seriousness with which the pastors and office staff approached everything indicated that they knew they were carrying heavy burdens. One thing Walt noticed right away was that the staff did not have much fun together. The church board, by contrast, underfunctioned by being content to sit back and act on recommendations from the staff without much committee consideration or planning. While the staff liked to joke about a pastor from the more distant past, affectionately nick-named "Pops," who was always the one left to empty trash cans and turn out the lights at the end of a long evening at church, no one among them was willing to relinquish any of his or her own serious responsibility for decisions and care for the church. The comfortable symmetry of the overfunctioners and the underfunctioners was a symptom of the balance that kept Old Hickory stuck in its inability to make transformative changes.

3. Blaming the church's problems on one person.

When changes are happening or need to happen in a congregation, frequently there are differences among members and leaders about how to address the changes. Because it is hard to acknowledge that a loving caring community or team will have real differences of opinion, the anxiety about change can drive the opposing sides to unite in focusing on one person or group who is obviously in need of lots of extra attention. We call this person the "identified problem person," to remind us that the problematic behavior actually points to some larger conflict. At Old Hickory Church some people jumped in to protect Jill and Don and began to blame all their troubles on Walt. Because of his temporary status and his willingness to ask hard questions and take firm stands, Walt quickly became the identified problem person.

However, the intensity of the conflicts around Jill and Don suggested that they had also become the projected problem for a more durable tension or anxiety in the system. On further reflection, Walt was able to identify three distinct, and very different, subgroups among the people he had come to know at Old Hickory, whose unresolved relationships were projected onto the staff and the interim pastor.

- Some of the members identified themselves as loyal to the mission of their denomination. They were involved in denominational programs and attended regional and national meetings and believed the church's main job was to be the best Protestants of their stripe.

- Others wore their denominational label very loosely and thought of themselves as a social group of friends. This group included members of small fellowship groups that had been meeting for more than twenty years. Others regularly made overseas trips together. For this second group, worship was a ritual they enjoyed as part of their regular fellowship — a time to be together and catch up with one another.

- A third group had gotten involved in a widely known Bible-study curriculum that promoted sharing of personal problems and deepening commitment to God. The fact that this Bible-study method espoused a theological perspective quite different from that promoted by the denomination, and that the fellowship created in the Bible study was exclusive to those who had attended the study groups, set the third group apart from the other two.

At least tacitly, each of these groups operated on a very different view of what church is and how church should operate. Instead of confronting each other with these differences, however, the three subchurch groups were able to come together to help their poor, overworked staff who were constantly in some kind of difficulty. The staff conflicts, Walt concluded, may just be a projection of the underlying conflict among the groups in the church. In fact, he thought to himself, it's very much like a family in which the children act out in order to bring together the parents whose marriage would otherwise be in serious difficulty. Instead of fighting with each other, Mom and Dad divert their anxieties to dealing with their "problem" children. In this way, Walt began to see the staff problems as symptoms pointing to a deeper reality in the life of Old Hickory.

4. **Physical or emotional impairment in key leaders.**

Certainly not every difficulty in key leaders is a symptom of something else going on in the system. The question of whether or not something is a symptom is worth asking, however. Walt considered that his cough that would not go away and was not part of his usual medical history might be a sign that he was getting too caught up in the anxiety of Old Hickory. It prompted him to look for metaphors and stories that connected to the difficulties that he was experiencing. He had a suspicion that his body was telling him the "air" was not healthy at Old Hickory Church and he was breathing way too much of it.

A related common "impairment" at Old Hickory was burnout. The staff members talked about burnout all the time. They worried about burned-out lay leaders. They even remembered how Pastor Morton had said he was burned out when he resigned years ago. Such heroic overfunctioning of the staff and such taking on of responsibility for matters that rightfully belong to others can definitely lead to weariness and discouragement. When the symptomatic issues of burnout are the focus of discussion, however, the congregation and staff easily miss the underlying issues that keep the whole congregation from addressing their fears and learning from their past.

The Issues of Power and Love Hiding behind the Symptoms

To bring hope and healing to a congregation, I encourage you to do some careful investigation to discover what else is going on in the church that is prompting such symptoms to arise. Under stress, your congregation is not able to articulate its deeper issues in direct, logical terms. Because the community of faith is so important to its members, and so intricately intertwined with their deepest existential concerns, the anxieties, desires, and fears that drive its relationships are typically expressed indirectly so as not to cause excessive hurt and disruption of community. Responding to these symptoms directly, as real and painful as they are, seldom moves a congregation to greater health and wholeness. So family systems theorists use the concept of metaphor to help detect the issues that are hiding behind the symptoms.

In the Old Hickory situation, we can see the tendency of members of the congregation to focus on the problems of the staff as a metaphor of the need to protect and care for these important members of the community. This concern is, however, quite intrusive and not considerate of the private lives of the staff members. At the same time the tendency of the congregation to encourage the staff members to work excessive hours on their behalf is also about controlling their lives. The Bible-study group exchanged love for control when it gave its members a shallow sense of intimacy in return for personal confession, moral supervision, and secrecy. The delicate power balance between the mission group, the social group, and the Bible-study group was carefully maintained through the belief that "we're just one big happy family." In fact, the congregation was stuck in these adaptive modes of life. The congregation

---

METAPHORS FOR
FRUSTRATED LOVE AND POWER

Behaviors	Metaphors for
Win-lose attitudes, use of terms such as "war" and "enemy"	Issues of control—who's going to be in charge here
Psychosomatic illness, self-destructive behavior, strong rivalries and antagonisms	Need to receive love/affection
Tendency toward "cultic" religion, or "the leader knows best" intrusive/abusive control	Desire for (and/or avoidance of) real love and intimacy

Source: Cloe Madanes, *Sex, Love and Violence* (New York: Norton, 1990).

could not rise to meet the changing needs of its members or the changes in society around it because any variation in congregational life was met by resistance from one group or another unwilling to give up the balances of power and control. Each effort of Interim Pastor Lindsey to address the symptoms by shifting the structures and stories toward more open policies and communication was met with increasing resentment from the leaders and the staff. He slowly learned that he had missed the metaphors of power and desire.

Metaphors for a Congregational Secret

You will want to keep in mind as you think about your own situation that the Old Hickory story is unique because of the presence of a secret in its life. Not all congregational conflicts are about secrets, but when the conflict resists the kinds of assessment I have demonstrated so far, it is worth asking if the symptoms could be metaphors for something carefully covered up. The forces at Old Hickory that held the congregation in its cycles of conflict were stronger than the collective forces of good people who wanted their church to be better than it was. Able people on the staff and bright capable people on the church board all desired their church to be strong and healthy. But they were stuck in a deeper impulse to protect the congregation and its constituency from the painful knowledge of sexual transgression by previous pastors. Many of the symptoms that were obvious "problems" to Walt and the personnel committee were metaphors for those secrets.

Congregations keep secrets on the assumption that doing so protects the members (and the public) from the pain of the information and the shame that such information brings. There is evidence, however, that the secret keeping is a benefit to the person in power who gets to keep his pride and status, while victims and members in general are hurting. Family therapist Candace Benyei has studied the issues of clergy misconduct and has concluded that "keeping of a secret produces more pain to more people than the original insult itself. This is because while the original wounding may have been a single incident or have involved a single victim, the keeping of the secret inevitably, over time, involves many people and repeated incidents of the above secret keeping behaviors."[3] Her experience in working with congregations has shown that a church may devote itself to hiding not only information about the incidents around the secret, but also hiding "the resultant rage, anger, loss, fear, and shame."[4]

Hope for Old Hickory

As leaders, we can take courage from the example of Walt Lindsey. When he learned to see that the symptoms at Old Hickory were likely metaphors for painful secrets and difficult power struggles, he recognized that the issues were beyond his ability to provide help. He persuaded the church board to bring in a local family therapist who was skilled in congregational consultation. Under her guidance a gathering of church leaders was able to discuss the church's history. Those conversations included the first ever open conversation about pastoral misbehavior. Members and leaders were able in that setting to draw some healing conclusions about their past. After three meetings with the consultant, they began to experience a resurgence of hope. With a fresh understanding of their situation, the board began to take charge of the financial and programmatic life of the church, and Jill and Don were freed to look for positions where they'd be happier in other churches in the metropolitan area. Former Pastor Morton quietly withdrew from Old Hickory Church and began worshiping in another congregation. At the close of the interim time, the church called a new pastor who was quite different from the charismatic and hierarchical pastors they'd had in the past, and who has enjoyed a fruitful ministry at Old Hickory for a good number of years.

By the grace of God, Old Hickory Church escaped the swamp of secrets and conflicted symptoms and re-created its structures

---

3. Candace R. Benyei, *Understanding Clergy Misconduct in Religious Systems: Scapegoating, Family Secrets and the Abuse of Power* (New York: Haworth Press, 1998), 104.

4. Ibid., 106.

in ways that allowed everyone to have fair access to power and decision-making. The three separate groups were acknowledged as different but belonging to a common community. The narrative of despair that leads to burnout was replaced with a story of hope that encouraged a more collaborative leadership that knew its limits and enjoyed the give and take of disagreements. With a more satisfactory structure and a more hopeful story, the symptoms receded into the background, and Old Hickory Church was able to negotiate the natural changes that confronted it from within and from the world around it. Learning from its symptoms brought new hope and new promise to a good congregation.

Reflection on Learning from Symptoms

1. As you reflect on your situation and the information you have identified on structures and stories, do you find the conflict continues to confuse you? Are key players continuing to resist open conversations?

2. What significant changes have recently taken place in your congregation? How does such experience of change relate to the presence of conflict?

3. Identify behaviors in your congregation that correspond to the types of symptoms mentioned in this chapter: emotion out of proportion, blaming or projection, over- and under-functioning, and leader impairment.

4. Name at least one metaphor that is symbolized by some of the symptoms you have identified in no. 3. What underlying reality does that metaphor represent?

5. To what extent do you think that the conflict in your congregation is related to a secret?

Chapter Six

Finding the Positive Purpose
of the Conflict

THE HOPEFUL HYPOTHESIS

Reflecting on the Mystery of Conflict

As the case of the "Kitchen Key" in chapter 1 showed, a common leadership mistake is to make a quick and simple diagnosis about what is wrong with the congregation, or its pastor, or its staff, or its most reactive or even villainous member. When we make a quick diagnosis, we then attempt to resolve the problem by addressing what is wrong. In this way of thinking, a diagnostic point of view prompts a leader to assume some sort of disease or malfunction has caused the conflict to erupt and to expect resolution by treating the disease.

Yet a trait shared by effective leaders is their refusal to make quick judgments about any situation. The more troubling the situation, the more important it is to look more deeply. When the leaders take time to reflect calmly and critically on the troubles of a congregation, they are more likely to find hope than discouragement. In the model I propose in this book, this time of critical reflection involves a search for the movement of God's Spirit in the congregation.

The Ugly Duckling Church

In one particular church, a hopeful hypothesis helped a leader stay calm, focused, and positive about the chaos and discouragement that accompanied and followed a particularly unpleasant period of the church's life. I call this congregation Ugly Ducking Church because when Suzanna Sennette arrived, the leaders and members of the church were quite certain theirs was the most unlovable, most conflict ridden, and least appealing church in the denomination. They were amazed that this pastor would agree to serve them during their time of transition.

Pastor Suzanna was well primed in the ways of wise, mature leadership described in chapter 8 of this book and began to minister to all of the people with a calm sense of confidence. She had experience serving in congregations during times of conflict and knew some ways to guide a congregation toward better health. This experience helped her to bring a large measure of care and love toward the members, no matter which side of the conflict they happened to be on.

The information that had been shared by the search committee was that the previous pastor, Roy Robinson, had lasted less than a year and a half because he was not a "good fit" for the congregation. Roy had understood that this was a very conservative church, and so he began preaching sermons about the hot-button issue of abortion. He railed against the liberal church establishment and denominational policies. Unfortunately, Roy had failed to read the culture of the congregation correctly. While most of the members were politically and fiscally conservative, they were not, by and large, strong advocates of biblical moralism and were open on issues of sexuality and women's concerns. In addition a number of moderate and liberal members of the congregation were openly shocked at Roy's pulpit position.

Suzanna heard the story of a so-called "secret society" that had formed in response to the rising dissatisfaction to try to get Roy to leave. Apparently the strategy worked, because Roy had let people in the congregation know that he felt he had been forced to leave. The identities of members of the secret society were not immediately revealed to Suzanna, but it was obvious that members of the church had chosen sides between those who wanted to "get rid" of the pastor and those who were angry at those who treated their pastor that way. With these stories as background, Suzanna began making careful observations and also continued asking members and the staff to tell their stories about how they saw things in the church.

Hopeful Reflection

In this model of conflict utilization, I encourage the leader to begin moving toward a hopeful hypothesis for a congregation with the observations he or she makes of the structures, stories, and symptoms in the conflicted congregation. To find hope, we learn to think about the conflict as reflecting God's transforming spirit at work in a congregation that is deeply interrelated. Reflection leading to the hypothesis does not find blame or fault in individuals or groups. Instead it assumes the congregation is responding to change in its own unique ways. In the case of the Ugly Duckling, Suzanna Sennette recognized that the congregation reacted to Pastor Roy so strongly because they so desperately needed to have a collaborative stake in the worship life of the congregation. Unfortunately they did not know how to go about it. Her early reflection turned to hope that the bright and capable lay leaders would eventually learn to take the roles that were rightly theirs.

For you as a leader, writing the hypothesis is a creative process that involves gathering information, listening both to the situation and to the intuitions of your own heart, praying for God's guidance, and letting your mind and heart arrive at a hopeful place. It is a place you might not have found without such intentional reflection. It requires imagination. It is a movement from fuzziness to clarity. The hypothesis Suzanna eventually devised followed her early observations into such a hopeful place. Here is her hopeful hypothesis.

> Ugly Duckling Church sought to recover the proper role of lay leadership in accord with the authority and balance of a representative church governance system. The conflict around Roy and how the church handled his departure alerts the observer to the fact that the congregation has not learned how to

assume legitimate lay leadership. In other words, the so-called secret society, the overfunctioning staff, and the congregation's discouragement when it all went poorly were all attempts to find ways to balance the involvement of lay leaders with the power of the clergy in a time of transition.

For another example of a hopeful hypothesis, see page 113.

Looking at Structures

To illustrate how Suzanna arrived at such a hypothesis we'll review the structures, stories, and symptoms of the Ugly Duckling congregation.

Suzanna's observations and the reports she received revealed a lot about the structures of the congregation. Nearly every member of the staff admitted to a heavy workload that suggested overfunctioning. To take only one example, no matter what time the pastor arrived at the church, or left, or came back in the evening or on Sunday, the office manager was always working at her desk. By contrast, the church's governing board spent a lot of time in unfocused discussion without ever accomplishing much. Some of the committees did not meet, or when they met found little to do besides talk. An overfunctioning staff and underfunctioning governing board indicates troubles that run deeper than the personality of the former pastor.

Listening to Stories

By listening to the stories people told her, Suzanna found further help in forming her hypothesis. One common story was about how Burt, the pastor who preceded Roy, had single-handedly "saved the church." The way they remembered it, the city was planning to widen the street in front of the church and in the process block the front entrance of the church. When Burt came, he declared that he would not let that happen and mobilized the church leadership to lobby the city council to change the road plans, and in the process revitalized the congregation, increasing the attendance, tripling the programs of ministry and service, and restoring the confidence of the church. A leader in industry before he followed his calling to become a minister, Burt had led with great enthusiasm and with a clear sense of direction about what the church should and should not do in every situation. The role of the church governing board, in fact, had been simply to convene to hear Burt's recommendations and to ratify them.

The experience of such a strong, charismatic, and directive pastor not only fails to prepare lay leaders to be self-reliant but also potentially creates a sense of inadequacy in the lay leadership that could even border on shame. In the case of the Ugly Duckling Church, the story they told themselves about Burt's "savior" role led them to experience difficulty in picking a successor to Burt. Some members of the search committee that brought Roy to the church told the story of how they had felt under great pressure from the congregation to get a pastor in place because they were afraid that without a "savior pastor" the church would quickly fall apart.

Learning from Symptoms

It is not hard for us as leaders to identify the symptoms of this congregation. Besides the obvious over- and underfunctioning, the congregation is nearly unanimous in blaming all their problems on Pastor Roy, making him the identified problem. Hardly anyone could acknowledge any fault in the church or its members in the conflict they had experienced. At the same time, the anger at Roy and the discouragement about the future of the church is definitely out of proportion to the underlying situation. Even more revealing is the division of the congregation into two very angry groups, some of whose members are no longer able to speak to members of the opposite group.

The following chapter will describe how to plan strategies and interventions based on a hopeful hypothesis. The rest of this chapter will follow Rev. Sennette as an example to all of us as leaders, to see how she was able to think creatively to build a systemic hypothesis about her church's situation.

The Theory of a Hopeful Frame

As the term is used here, a "hypothesis" is a tentative, disprovable, adaptable working model of the functioning of a congregation as an interconnected web of relationships. A hypothesis differs from a diagnosis in that it is framed in a positive way. It seeks to define how and why the distortions of structure, narrative, or symptom seen in the congregation actually serve to keep the system in balance at the present time. The hypothesis also needs to be able to identify where health or maturity resides in the conflicted system. These concerns help a leader remember that conflict is not, in itself, a bad thing. Most often, a congregation falls into conflict because the transformation God seeks for it or its members in the present situation has been thwarted, or the natural adaptive mechanisms of the congregation are stuck on some problem or issue. Examples include: (1) a congregation with an aging membership is challenged by a younger generation with a request to meet the contemporary needs of that group, (2) a change in the demographics of the congregation's neighborhood tests its adaptive ability, or (3) a transition in pastoral leadership raises anxiety over the identity of the group or tension among competing groups for control of the congregation in a new chapter of its life. The tension between the need for a positive hypothesis and the possible presence of genuine destructive behavior or even cruel or malevolent intent is addressed later in this chapter. *In all this, learning how to seek the inner wisdom and health of the congregation through a hopeful hypothesis takes precedence over dealing with possible evil.*

Family systems theorists have generally encouraged a focus on health rather than disease.[1] Family theorists recognize that conflicts and symptoms are not simply causes or directly linear effects

---

1. Virginia Satir summarized the argument this way: "I feel that working on pathology is like beating a dead horse: no life is there. I don't believe that we have much to show for the uncountable hours spent in the aggregate by all the helpers in the world who have approached therapy from a pathological orientation. In these days of holistic health thinking, biofeedback, visual imagery, right-left brain integration, we can no longer see or behave as we did. I have seen over time the real advantages of looking at things from a health oriented perspective." "A Partial Portrait of a Family Therapist in Process," in *Evolving Models for Family Change:*

of problems or disease in the system. Instead problems are indi-
cations of what family systems theorist Lynn Hoffman called "a
dilemma faced by a family on its evolutionary path."[2] Recognizing
that change of any kind tends to unbalance or destabilize a human
system, a family theorist who uses hypotheses extensively[3] suggests
three particular ways that problems or symptoms serve a family in
positive ways:

- All symptoms in children stabilize unstable marriages, and if a
  "small symptom" cannot stabilize a marriage, then a "larger
  symptom" will be needed.

- The greater the magnitude of the marital conflict, the greater will
  be the magnitude of the symptom.

- The more covert or hidden the marital conflict, the more a symptom will be needed to stabilize the marital conflict so it can
  remain hidden or covert.

By changing a few words in these assumptions, we can easily see
parallels to how conflict in a church can serve a positive purpose —
at least in the short term:

- All symptoms, whether in key leaders or significant groups or
  structures, serve to stabilize unstable congregational dynamics.
  It does not matter if the symptoms in key leaders are related to
  instability in their own families, the parallel process works to
  stabilize the congregation as well. If a small symptom cannot
  stabilize a congregation, a larger symptom will be needed.

- The greater the magnitude of conflict within a congregation, the
  greater the needed magnitude of symptoms in key leaders or
  structures.

A Volume in Honor of Salvador Minuchin, ed. H. Charles Fishman and Bernice
Rosman (New York: Guilford Press, 1986), 291.

2. Lynn Hoffman, *Foundations of Family Therapy: A Conceptual Framework
for Systems Change* (New York: Basic Books, 1981), 347.

3. Joel Bergman, *Fishing for Barracuda: Pragmatics of Brief Systemic Therapy*
(New York: W. W. Norton, 1985), 4.

♦ The more covert or hidden the congregational conflict, the more a symptom will be needed in key figures to stabilize the congregational conflict so it can remain hidden.

A major attraction of family systems theory is its hopefulness about conflict and change. It explains how conflict arises from the developmental and evolutionary fluctuations working from within a family or other human system, as well as the social and political forces of change impacting the family from outside. Conflict may accompany either the tension brought about by the transformation that is happening or about to happen, or attend a system that needs to change to adapt and survive but that is stuck in its current comfortable ways of functioning. When transformation is happening, the conflict reveals the turmoil and sometimes the chaos of a system in change. As Heifetz and Linsky point out, change means the loss of cherished "habits, values and attitudes" which, even if they have stopped being helpful in themselves, are deeply tied to the identity of those who hold them.[4] The loss of identity that comes with change brings with it a sense of disloyalty toward those who fostered that identity in the first place. The turmoil of change is a natural struggle of the members of the system to maintain some continuity when everything is changing around them. Another way of describing the conflict that arises from change is that it reflects the "righting of the boat." In sailing, particularly, whenever the boat turns, there is some experience of instability until the boat has regained its balance in the new direction.

The Theology of a Positive Hypothesis

From a perspective within the Christian faith, change is seen as the way God's creative spirit works in human life. The call to repentance is all about transformation. The invitation to grow or mature in the faith is about change. Following God's call entails adapting human

---

4. Ronald A. Heifetz and Marty Linsky, *Leadership on the Line: Staying Alive through the Dangers of Leading* (Cambridge, MA: Harvard Business School Press, 2002), 26ff.

behavior to a divine demand. Jesus' proclamation that everything is made new in him reminds us of the transformation that happens in human life when God's spirit enters in. The theology behind the inner wisdom approach to congregational conflict is a theology of transformation. God is incarnate in the structures of a congregation; God's Word is articulated in its stories; the transformation God is calling for is revealed in the symptoms as the church is either stuck or unbalanced by the change.

When change is resisted, when God's call for transformation is being frustrated, the symptoms of conflict can be seen as helpful reminders of that resistance. I like to describe this process through a family metaphor. Imagine a family with little children, of preschool and early elementary age. At some point the parent or parents recognize the need for some structure and so they set a rule about bedtime for the children. Let's say they establish 8:00 p.m. as the rule, and they begin enforcing the rule by having snacks eaten, baths taken, sleepwear put on, teeth brushed, and bedtime stories and prayers completed in time for an eight o'clock "lights out" time. Adults usually find this very liberating, and children usually find they are better rested and happier with some clear structures for their lives. As the children in this family get older, the parent or parents insist on continuing to enforce the eight o'clock rule with the saying, "This is the way things are in this family." The rule, of course, gets harder to enforce as the children grow toward their teens. If the rule continues to be strictly enforced into the teen years, however, trouble will sooner or later rear its head. The young adults will begin to rebel or act out in some way against the rule and its enforcers. Some may assume that such teens are "bad kids" because of their unruly behavior. From a systems perspective quite the opposite is clear. The teen members of the family are playing a positive role to alert the family and the support system for that family that the family needs to change, to grow, to adapt. Instead of something bad, the conflict is a good warning signal to the family to adapt its rules to the developmental changes that naturally occur in their children or face even worse conflict. Developmental changes are one way God prompts us to be transformed. The family turmoil points to the deep inner wisdom of the family that needs to change. The conflict points to the inner wisdom of the congregation needing both change and continuity.

The way a wise, mature leader can make a difference in a conflicted situation is to find the positive function of the conflict. A hopeful hypothesis is the model for such discovery. It needs to be phrased in such a way that it proposes an answer to the question, "How does the symptom serve the overall health of the congregation?" Or it might address the question: "How does the conflict point to the transformation God desires for the congregation?" The assumption is that the conflict is about the tensions of the change or the result of human resistance to the transformation. The leader needs to think in a humble and positive way, through a systemic hypothesis. Otherwise the congregation will resist the insights and leadership because the system will hear the leader as being judgmental or critical. The way of love is to find the hope.[5]

This emphasis on hopeful frames for uncomfortable realities does not eliminate the need to recognize that destructive behavior on the part of individuals or groups exists. Nor does this emphasis condone such bad behavior. Abusive behavior, destructive acting out on property or persons, or talk in the congregation that deceives, slanders, divides, confuses, or works against the mission of the church needs to be stopped. A saying attributed to Archbishop Desmond Tutu says that a mouse does not appreciate neutrality when its tail

---

5. The actual truth claim of the hypothesis is set aside for the purpose of the research or investigation. Because churches in trouble are often as difficult and resistive as very troubled families, it is helpful to seek health and hope rather than malfunction and disease by creating a hypothesis. After looking at structures, listening to stories, and learning from symptoms, a leader can benefit from a statement that brings all of the confusing information together and organizes it to bring meaning to the sometimes absurd realities of conflict. The hypothesis statement might be very simple and even elegant in its simplicity, or it might be more complex to reflect the many layers of relationships and intricacies of connections in the system. As in the practice of scientific research, any hypothesis is always tentative, based on the theory and limited knowledge available at any time. A good investigator always stands ready to find a hypothesis disproved by further data, or adapted to new insights gained from working in the system. Like a researcher, the leader of a congregation in conflict follows a circular process that moves from hypothesis to strategy to intervention and then back to revise the hypothesis based on how the intervention worked or did not work.

is under an elephant's foot. Discussions of strategy in a later chapter will include ways to take action to prevent abuse and protect its victims. Nonetheless, a positive, tough-loving approach, even to the abuser, will always be more effective.

Creating a Hopeful Hypothesis for Ugly Duckling Church

When a leader hears a predominance of negative information in the structures and stories and symptoms, as Pastor Sennette did in the case of the Ugly Duckling congregation, she needs to spend extra time reflecting and trying to find the inner wisdom of a system that thought it had precious little. She recognizes that unless a positive frame shapes the pastor's thinking and work, the congregation will continue in their much-diminished self-esteem.

On the surface the congregation appeared to be burdened with some strong-willed lay leaders who tended to follow their own agendas rather than the well-being of the church. The congregation seemed to present itself as one of those that select the polar opposite of the previous pastor and then blame that new pastor for not being more like the predecessor. The level of anger and hurt with lots of blaming and many broken relationships in the congregation indicated a high level of persistent and resistant conflict. But the pastor looked beyond these presenting problems and the surface turbulence they represented. After a few weeks, people began to tell the stories behind the symptoms. The following points summarize a few of them:

- A member of the so-called secret society came to Rev. Sennette to tell her "side" of the story. As she described it, there was only one meeting of a group of leaders who had gathered out of their deep love of the church to try to find a way to keep their church from getting into further conflict and trouble. When Pastor Roy announced his resignation, his supporters heard about that meeting and the story became inflated until it was known as a "secret society."

- As Rev. Sennette got to know the staff members, it became clear that none of them was jealously guarding their work as a special fiefdom of accumulated power. It turned out that they were busily burning themselves out because they loved the church and wanted everything to go well, never stopping to think that their overwork contributed to the lack of involvement of the lay leaders.

- Expecting to find a long history of squabbling and disputes, Rev. Sennette discovered that the history of the church was blessed with few conflicts, and none that had seriously damaged the church and its unity. It appeared that the congregation had seriously undervalued its own worth primarily because, without other conflicts to compare to this one, their current problems seemed worse than they actually were.

Discoveries such as these helped Rev. Sennette to build a more positive statement about how the conflict with Roy served to balance the congregation. Here again is the statement she constructed as a "hopeful hypothesis":

> Ugly Duckling Church sought to recover the proper role of lay leadership in accord with the authority and balance of a representative church governance system. The conflict around Roy and how the church handled his departure alerts the observer to the fact that the congregation has not learned how to assume legitimate lay leadership. In other words, the so-called secret society, the overfunctioning staff, and the congregation's discouragement when it all went poorly were all attempts to find ways to balance the involvement of lay leaders with the power of the clergy in a time of transition.

This statement puts the central difficulties in the positive light of the struggle of the church to keep itself in balance amid all the changes it was experiencing. The hypothesis brings to bear the formal sources of health of the church in its denominational tradition on its desire to use the many talents of its lay leaders. At the same time the hypothesis shows how the very things most folks thought were terrible actions and inevitable reactions were actually done in the service of the overall health and welfare of the church.

As a church leader, you probably recognized fairly quickly that this congregation was quite remarkable in the quality of its local program and the depth of its commitment to the denomination's missionary enterprises. Furthermore, Rev. Sennette noticed that the members of the congregation, with only a couple of exceptions, were amiable, non-confrontational people who were better at church fellowship and mission than they were at church conflict. The congregation was in reality more like a lovely and graceful swan than an ugly duckling.

Working from a hypothesis like this one, a leader is able to use the structures and the stories of the congregation to encourage the resources of health in the system to overcome the symptoms of conflict.

This hopeful hypothesis works on three levels of interaction in the congregational system. First, it helps the leader to keep the inner wisdom of the system in mind when responding to the stresses and anxieties of a congregation in conflict. Knowing that something positive was working in the system resonates with the faith and hope that we can tap our inner sage for wise advice on the way to stay true to ourselves and to God in the situation.

Second, although the hypothesis can be shared selectively with others in the system,[6] the positive nature of the hypothesis helps leaders to act in loving and respectful ways for everyone in the system, even the most irritating. Knowing that the key players in the difficulties are probably bearing symptoms of the deeper change

---

6. Ordinarily the hypothesis is known only to the leader and the team working the conflict. In a contractual relationship between an outside leader and a congregation, the hypothesis can be shared with either the internal conflict task force or the church board, depending on the contract. The level of reactivity of any individual or group is the criterion for sharing the hypothesis. In situations like Old Hickory Church in chapter 5 and Mission Church in chapter 7 most church members and leaders were too reactive to be able to hear a hypothesis until after the family therapist was brought into the situation. In the Ugly Duckling Church, Rev. Sennette began to share the hypothesis with mature leaders who could become collaborators with her in moving the church toward greater health.

toward health in the system allows us to hold a more positive attitude. For most of the key players in the system who see themselves on one side or another of a conflicted situation, personal reflection and change is easier to consider when they know they are loved and respected by their leaders.

And finally, even if the hypothesis may not be the best or most accurate reading of the situation, it seeks to ally itself with the health (rather than sickness or incapacity) of the system, which elicits more change and growth toward health in the congregation.

Looking for Health

This chapter has not yet indicated what exactly is meant by "health" in the context of a systemic perspective on congregational life. As a leader, what exactly should you look for in order to uncover the health in a system that appears unhealthy? We know that not all change is good, and not all conflict leads to more health.

Definition of Health in This Work

Drawing on the process theology of Henry Nelson Wieman, we can identify four dimensions of health.[7] Believing that God calls each church to liberating, creative transformation, indicators of progress toward transformation are:

+ increased knowledge and expanding awareness of truth,

+ increased respect for the dignity of difference among persons,

+ deepening of community among its members and between members and those outside the system, and

+ growing ability for members to take positive mutual action in response to events.

Increased knowledge and expanding awareness of truth indicates that people are listening and hearing each other in the context of conflict. Someone has said that truth is so precious that each of us

7. Bruce Southworth, *At Home in Creativity: The Naturalistic Theology of Henry Nelson Wieman* (Boston: Skinner House Books, 1995), 42.

has to recognize that we have only a small part of it. We have to be willing to hear and learn from people with other perspectives in order to gain more of the truth. Open minds are best in a conflict. If minds are not open, at the very least they can be humble and recognize that they might have missed something along the way and may not be right. Of course when people start choosing sides in a conflict, they tend to assume that their side is right and the others are wrong. They come to fear that if they admit that the opposite side's argument has any validity, they would set themselves up to lose the contest and thus would be disloyal to their "side." From the example of the Ugly Duckling congregation we see that the perception of a "secret society" was an indicator of such a loss of health in the system. Some members and key leaders assumed that that group had kept their meetings secret in order to keep "the other side" from getting information about what was happening. By refusing to ask open, honest questions, and by refusing to gather information that might differ from their emotional perceptions, they were diminishing rather than expanding their base of knowledge and deliberately avoiding an encounter with the truth. Rev. Sennette found another indicator of lack of health in the Ugly Duckling Church in the readiness of some members to blame Pastor Roy for all of their problems and to deny that the congregation played any role in creating the problems as they developed. Denial is another way of diminishing knowledge in individuals and in larger groups. Simple common sense would indicate that it takes two sides to make a conflict, and that the congregation as a whole and some of the leaders in particular had behaved in ways that led to the conflict. If they had allowed themselves to wonder why they had chosen Roy in the first place, with all the evidence that he did not have the kind of personality that would be a good fit for the church's needs, they might have grown in knowledge and wisdom. Furthermore, they would have recognized that they had failed to hold Roy accountable for his performance as a pastor in a loving and effective way. Instead of reacting with letters of complaint when he did things they did not like, they might have found constructive ways to communicate their concerns. The failure of the leaders of the congregation to take positive action to remedy the difficulties when they first appeared played a major part in the escalation of the conflict that led to Roy's departure. If the congregation persists in denying their role in the history of Roy's pastorate, they will not be able to examine facts and grow in knowledge in order to learn healthier ways to handle conflict in the future. When a leader is able to help a congregation face the truth and increase knowledge about their situation and about each other, God's change can happen.

Increased respect for the dignity of difference among persons[8] is seldom recognized as an indicator of creative change in a church. A common desire of congregations is for sameness in values, attitudes, and beliefs. Certainly we're more comfortable with each other when we see more of what we have in common than ways we are different. That comfort zone is disturbed when we discover that we may be different in significant ways. In churches with a strong comfort zone of homogeneity, signs of difference are seen as signs of trouble. When those differences evolve into conflict, the immediate conclusion is that there's something wrong with "them" because they're different. Members long for the good old days when everyone seemed more alike and harmony apparently reigned.

This fear of difference contributed to the escalation of the conflict at the Ugly Duckling Church. A congregation that thought they were a harmonious unity discovered that they had differing expectations of their pastor and a variety of responses to the pastor's style. The fear of difference made their problems seem bigger than they were. If the congregation had learned earlier that it was acceptable to listen carefully to each other and recognize that there might be more than one way to interpret a situation, they might have weathered the difficulties with Pastor Roy.

Deepening of community can be a genuine indicator of healthy and creative change in a congregation. When change happens with the expected turbulence that surrounds it and people find themselves moving through the turbulence with a greater love and appreciation

---

8. Jonathan Sachs, *The Dignity of Difference: How to Avoid the Clash of Civilizations* (London: Continuum Books, 2002).

for their fellow members and an increased desire to worship, study, pray, serve, and socialize with each other, the change has been for the good. If the results of change bring a decrease in trust, irreconcilable difficulties, or increased distance from each other, then the change has not been healthy. An example of deepening community can be seen in the response of one congregation to their pastor's being diagnosed with cancer. The pastor, to her credit, was able to be open with the congregation about the illness and the progress of the treatment. The congregation, for its part, was able to rally around the pastor and give her the kinds of support she needed during her therapy. On the Sunday that her hair had fallen out from the chemotherapy, everyone came to church with a hat on as a sign of solidarity with the pastor. The flexibility and caring of that community was even more remarkable because the founding pastor of that congregation had died of cancer while in office, and it was a long-remembered difficulty. But their action in the present had a healing effect. The congregation grew in their faith and in their care and love for each other and for their pastor. They faced change and made something positive out of it.

A growing ability for members to take positive mutual action in response to events. Reverend Sennette found that the congregation was stymied in their ability to take action. They were so angry at each other and so traumatized by the flare-up of conflict among them that they could not imagine themselves working to solve any problems as they arose. When the church bus broke down and some decision needed to be made about either getting it repaired or selling it and purchasing another, the church board talked endlessly about the bus but could not arrive at a conclusion. After the first year with Rev. Sennette, however, the board had grown in confidence and had accepted its formal authority. The board reconsidered the issue of the church bus and within a few minutes of discussion was able to decide to spend the extra money repairing the bus so that both the emotional attachment the youth group had to that bus and the environmental impact of junking such a vehicle could be addressed constructively.

Qualities of a Good Hopeful Hypothesis

With these criteria for health in a transforming situation, the leader can imagine a hopeful hypothesis that finds and encourages the health in the system. The conflict itself, rather than a destructive event in the history of the congregation, begins to be seen as a constructive, creative way to try to solve the emerging issues of change. The hypothesis is an organizing tool, offering the leaders involved, and perhaps the whole system, a "scaffolding on which to hang the masses of information thrown out" by the members of the congregation. It provides a "thread to follow" in moving through the chaos of a conflict situation.[9] The positive, hopeful nature of the hypothesis "is at once paradoxical and confusing to [system] members. Symptoms are not criticized or defined as undesirable in any way. Symptoms, as well as all the behaviors of all [system] members, are punctuated as important to the well-being and cohesion" of the church and its members.[10] There is no room for the word "dysfunctional" and there is no judgment. Instead the hypothesis offers hope.

A hypothesis works best if it:

* Brings more knowledge to the situation. This means that the hypothesis has to ring true to the one creating the hypothesis and to other members of the system. This does not mean the statement is necessarily the "only truth" about the situation, or the absolute truth. The hypothesis continues to be tentative and disprovable, but it must correspond to what is known and recognized about the situation. Sometimes a leader is tempted to create a fictitious frame for the situation in order to bring hope where little is to be found. It is better, however, to dig deeper in the information of the situation and in the imagination to create a hypothesis that is as real as possible.

* Recognizes that there are real and painful differences among the members of the congregation. The hypothesis acknowledges

---

9. Hoffman, *Foundations of Family Therapy*, 294.
10. Becvar and Becvar, *Family Therapy*, 252.

these differences and frames them in positive ways to recognize that people of integrity differ, often out of their deeper commitment and care for the congregation. A good hypothesis is positive for as many members of the system as possible, on whichever "side" of the conflict they might find themselves. It needs to offer hope to all, not just to those on one side or another.

+ Is fully relational. The hypothesis assumes that there are no isolated individual issues in the situation, but that everything is related to everything else. A deep belonging to a circle of interrelatedness exists in and around the congregation, and the patterns of the conflict are connected to that circle.

+ Leads to a positive strategy that provides a fair opportunity for everyone to participate in moving the congregation toward the transformation at hand. Simple solutions based on singling out individuals or taking sides will not promote healthy transformation. The next chapter will spell out strategies in more detail.

Loving Leadership

With a creative, positive, hopeful hypothesis a leader of a congregation in conflict gains a powerful leverage point to make a difference. A hopeful hypothesis fuels the leader with both a love for the whole situation and a vantage point beyond the situation that provides a perspective of health. The leverage comes from the slight edge that love has over hate in the world. The perspective allows a person to engage in loving confrontation of the unloving, unconstructive behaviors of others without needing to judge or divide. At any given moment, the awareness of a hopeful hypothesis may serve to keep a leader from giving up on the situation or choosing unhelpful or unwise behaviors in an attempt to salvage the situation single-handedly. The love that Suzanna Sennette brought to the Ugly Duckling congregation helped her to spend most of her time and energy on the positive possibilities in the congregation. She was able to wait patiently for the members of the congregation to catch the vision of the goodness and health that were there. Her closest friends would acknowledge that there were times when she wanted to give it all up and other times when she was ready to take unilateral action to intervene in some emerging crisis or another. But mostly, the act of remembering the real, deep need of the congregation to affirm and empower the talented lay leadership to meet the challenges of their present situation helped her to remain calm, loving, and hopeful. The members of the church formerly known as the Ugly Duckling congregation agreed that she played her role exactly the way they needed her to do.

Reflection on the Hopeful Hypothesis

1. Take some quiet time and gather your thoughts about the structures, stories, and symptoms of your situation. Allow your mind and your heart to search for the positive function that the conflict is playing in the life of the congregation.

2. Write a draft of a hopeful hypothesis for your situation.

3. Review the qualities of a positive hypothesis and edit or rewrite your hypothesis to make it more open to knowledge, more truthful about the difficulties, more relational and loving, and more likely to suggest positive strategies.

4. If you have conversation partners, show them your hypothesis and ask them to critique it based on their insights as leaders.

Chapter Seven

Challenging the System to Evoke the Hope

The Hidden Issues at Mission Church

The conflict at the Mission Community Church came to the attention of the judicatory when Frank Braddock, the pastor of three years, came under fire from key leaders in the congregation. After a brief consultation between the judicatory and the congregation, Frank negotiated a termination contract and left. An interim pastor, Gayla Durant, came to Mission with the understanding that she would be working with the judicatory conflict team with the hope of bringing greater health to the situation before a new pastor would start to work.

By looking at structures, listening to stories, and learning from symptoms, the conflict team had discovered several important elements about the way the Mission congregation defined their life together.

Structures

- The governing board of the church functioned very informally. Several of the committees did not meet, or met primarily for drinks and conversations in someone's home. The meetings of the governing board usually started late, following conversations around the coffee pot, and much of the meeting was devoted to solving minor church building or program problems presented by one elder or another.

- The congregation had a longstanding informal arrangement with "The Brotherhood of Man" (usually referred to as BOM), a non-profit social service agency that used space in the Mission Church building. Boundaries between the agency and the church were difficult to identify and seldom honored. The director of that agency, Geoff Abbot, was a minister of another denomination who, having served for ten years at Brotherhood, was often perceived as one of the pastors of the Mission congregation. Abbot regularly shared leadership in worship, preached once a month, and frequently performed weddings and funerals for Mission members who "knew Geoff better than the new pastor." This pattern continued after Interim Pastor Durant arrived. This fuzzy mix of roles was a potential problem for the successful entrance and service of the interim pastor. Another boundaries issue was the spillover of BOM's clothing distribution and pre-school programs that used the same "all-purpose room" that Mission Church used for worship. Frequently sorting operations and children's equipment were not out of the way in time for Sunday mornings.

Stories

* The self-description of the congregation was that they were a happy, loving community of friends and neighbors. The leaders had denied any possibility of differences among them and expressed confusion as to why they seemed to be divided over Pastor Braddock's ministry. Ordinarily they had fun together and were committed to the church's mission of community service.

* The pastor who had done the most to shape that congregation, Rev. Jerry Brown, had served for twenty years. When he left just four years earlier, he had refused to participate in any ritual ways of saying goodbye. Although he lived in a different state at the time of this case study, he continued to be in touch with many of his friends in the Mission Church. Not surprisingly, there was no effective transition work done between the time the beloved longtime pastor left and the time that Frank Braddock arrived.

Symptoms

♦ The complaints about Frank Braddock turned out to be about relatively unimportant issues. The consultants had observed that Frank had become more distant and less responsive to the members of the congregation during the time of the conflict, but hardly enough to warrant his dismissal. His preaching ministry had been consistent from the time he arrived, so concerns that he was too liberal for the members' tastes, while probably accurate, were not new and did not seem to be enough to cause the kind of anger that had been generated against him. It appeared that Braddock had become the identified problem in an unhealthy triangle between factions in the church and their new pastor.

♦ Members of key families had been the leaders of the campaign to get rid of Pastor Braddock. The consultants discovered that many of those same families had been and still were close to their previous pastor — a sign of another unresolved unhealthy triangle.

These were some of the factors the conflict team and the interim pastor considered as they sought to help the Mission Church move through the conflict toward health. None of these factors, taken by themselves or even together, adequately explained the intensity of the conflict that had led to Rev. Braddock's departure.

Using Conflict to Promote Change

The conflict team faced both immediate obstacles and long-term difficulties in seeking to bring hope and health to Mission Church. In the short run, they were working against a "quick fix" mentality that expected Braddock's departure to solve the problems of the church. To suggest otherwise, of course, would imply that there was something wrong with the congregation and that the judicatory was sitting in judgment over the leaders at Mission. The team had to find a positive frame for their continued partnership with the congregation. Over the long run, they needed a frame for their work that would allow them to explore and uncover the hidden difficulties and guide the church toward the kinds of changes God desired for them.

These concerns had to be addressed through a hopeful hypothesis. The question to be answered was: "In what way does this conflict serve to keep the congregation in balance, either in response to a change that is underway or out of frustration with the difficulty of adapting sufficiently for healthy transformation?" The hopeful hypothesis can create a bridge to a resistant group by honoring what is good and healthy in the congregation, and can also provide the path to further study and intervention. The "hopeful hypothesis" on which the team based their work with Rev. Durant and the Mission congregation is as follows.

> Mission Community Church is in a transitional phase of its story, needing to grow up into a new stage of maturity as a congregation, with more independence and freedom to go its own unique direction in its life, but also anxious about leaving behind the ties to the former pastor and his vision and programs. The Brotherhood of Man agency is also in a transitional phase and the tension between the two organizations, utilizing the same space, is inhibiting both of them from their fullest potential. The congregation engaged in conflict with Rev. Braddock out of loyalty to both Rev. Brown and to the partnership with Brotherhood, to hold on for another season to the comfort and excitement of that kind of collaboration for service to the community. New forms and new stories will be needed to move into the next chapter of Mission's life.

The Hopeful Challenges

Leaders wanting to use the conflict they experience in their congregations need to find ways to challenge the presenting issues and commonly agreed on structures, stories, and symptoms. Such challenges call into question in accepting and loving ways the definitions of the problems and the solutions tried. Using Mission Church as an example, leaders will note that the congregation was in deep trouble at the time the interim pastor and the conflict team came into the picture. Despite the story line that the congregation was a "happy family," the team discovered that the congregation and its leaders had not been functioning at their best for the past few years. The leaders' task was to confront Mission Church to find the hidden possibilities for health that existed in their identity. This led to challenges to the structures (the ways the congregation had organized itself, its patterns of relationship), the stories (the meanings the congregation gave to their life together), and the symptoms (signs that something else is going on) presented in the situation. To the extent the skills of the conflict team permitted, the challenges were based on the hopeful hypothesis and couched in ways that honored the spirit of the congregation.

Challenging the Structures

As the first effort at intervention, several structural challenges were considered by the conflict team as they reflected on ways to help get Mission Church back to its full potential. They ranged from simple observational challenges of naming and mapping, to identifying and supporting healthy structures where they were found, to more intrusive challenges such as rebalancing power inequities and experimenting with different structures.

Naming the Structures. The predominance of informal structures was the most obvious characteristic of the ways Mission Church had organized itself over the years. Even for a relatively small, family-sized congregation, the degree of informality was unusual. The official board meetings were hard to move from the coffee pot to the meeting table, and few committees worked to consider programs or problems ahead of the board's consideration. If everything else had been going well, the lack of formal meeting protocols and accountability might have been acceptable, but since the conflict had overwhelmed the ability of the leaders to make decisions and solve problems, the team encouraged Gayla to challenge the informality and find more formal ways to carry on the organizational work of the church. She began to insist on regular meeting times, more careful observance of the "rules of order" for meetings, and clearer accountability between the board and its committees. She also began to work with the secretary of the board and the church treasurer to keep better records of meetings and provide more adequate reports of the church's finances for the board's oversight.

A second structural challenge concerned the matter of boundaries. The team observed that the collaboration between the church and Brotherhood, the community service agency, was highly fluid and few distinctions were made between the work of the congregation and the organizational life of the agency. The two organizations had developed a creative and cooperative relationship over the years that had worked well in the early phases of their lives together. The team came to believe that as both the church and the agency matured these collaborative ties and the interweaving of their organizational boundaries had begun to show signs of strain. Informal mutuality had given way to power struggles, collegial reciprocity had moved to a rigid expectation of privileges, largely on the part of the agency, and a healthy interdependence had regressed to less healthy savior/victim relationships.[1] The fluid and permeable boundaries, while helpful in the early stages, appeared to have outlived their helpfulness. The mutual support and encouragement that was part of the original arrangement had been lost in the anxieties of change and survival of each institution with different leaders. Without trying to impose prescribed structures, the team decided to challenge the actual working structures of the situation. The way the relationship between the church and BOM was structured, without clear roles or boundaries, did not appear to be helping either organization or the members of the church to flourish.

Mapping. For its own interpretation the team worked up a structural map of the relationships in the Mission situation (see the map on the following page; see page 47 for an explanation of the symbols used). In interviews with leaders and members, the team had picked up additional information that went into the map. For example,

---

1. Thelma Jean Goodrich et al., *Feminist Family Therapy: A Casebook* (New York: Norton, 1988), 20.

STRUCTURAL MAP OF MISSION CHURCH

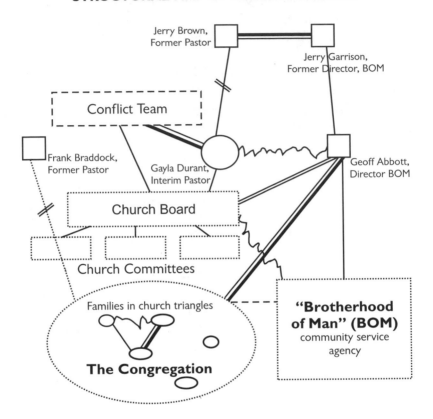

they had heard stories about the previous pastor, Jerry Brown, and about his partnership with Jerry Garrison, the founder of the Brotherhood of Man. Their friendship had enabled an informal and collaborative relationship to develop between the congregation and the agency, largely on a mutual understanding and without formal agreements or contracts. As long as both men were in their positions, the relationships flourished and benefited everyone. After Jerry Garrison left and Geoff Abbott became the director of BOM, the informal relationships continued with Geoff assuming a "junior" relationship to Jerry Brown. When Jerry Brown left, both the agency and the congregation transferred their expectations of leadership (and pastoral care) to Geoff, who became the informal "senior" pastor of Mission Church. Thus the map shows strong double lines of relationship between Geoff and the congregation. The initiative of Gayla to reassert the pastoral authority for herself then becomes a source of friction between herself and Geoff.

The presence of the Brotherhood of Man agency is shown as a large rectangle on the map because it is a full-service agency with a separate board and staff, and because it has grown to be a strong presence in the community and a large influence in the life of Mission Church. The wavy lines between BOM and the church board indicate the increasing demands, power struggles, and overfunctioning from the BOM side of the relationship, with complementary compliance, frustration, and sense of victimization on the congregation's side.

The large circle representing the congregation includes smaller ovals representing individual families as subsystems of the congregation. By parallel process, the conflict team was able to confirm that tensions among the families of the church existed in forms of triangles and strong emotional reactivity that was mirrored in the relationships between the congregation and former Pastor Braddock.

As Gayla began her work at Mission, she provided some "in-service" training to the members of the church board. In one of the early training modules she introduced the board to the concepts of structures and invited them to map the structures of their congregational organization. The board gained some new insight about their functioning as a board and several of them were encouraged to take more leadership in the congregation based on what they saw in the map they produced. Other members of the board disagreed, saying that the structures were not in harmony with the way everyone thought things were working at the church, and they came to the defense of the working relationship between the church and BOM. That particular training module had to be terminated because the emotions it aroused were quite intense, and board members were afraid they would get into more conflict as a result of that

conversation. Reflecting on that outcome, Gayla and the team decided not to do more direct naming and mapping interventions. The
team recognized that it was best to move to more indirect interventions, knowing that in highly emotional conflict situations there are
limits to the benefits of insight.

Reinforcing Healthy Structures. The next most positive intervention in the structural mode is finding and encouraging or
reinforcing the healthy structures that already exist in the church.
Interim Pastor Durant found a couple of pockets of health right
away and began to encourage them.

The adult education program was a highlight of strength and
flexibility at Mission. A small task force of three had been organizing the classes for adults on Sunday mornings and on Wednesday
evenings. They immediately sought out their new interim pastor and
asked for her suggestions and ideas. They let her know what was already planned for the coming quarter, and had many plans in place
for the rest of the year. Gayla rejoiced with them that attendance
had held up for these events through the worst of the conflict and
enjoyed the intellectual rigor and curiosity that this trio brought to
their tasks. Based on their interests and what Gayla knew of the
congregation, she made a few suggestions of resources and people
she knew who might fit into future plans, and she also offered to
teach a course on healthy family relationships based on her recent
studies in family therapy. That idea was welcomed by the planning
team and scheduled for later in that year. Gayla's expectation was
that reflection on matters of faith and current issues of ethics and
social justice would continue to be a balancing factor in moving
Mission Church toward greater health.

Rebalancing Power Inequities. What had begun as a collaborative leadership project, the church and the agency working together
under the friendly comradeship of the two Jerries, had become a
rigid exercise in privilege and nearly Gnostic insider knowledge.
Neither Frank Braddock nor Gayla Durant were to be considered
anything but subordinates to Geoff Abbott, and the church's life
was of secondary importance to that of the Brotherhood of Man

community service agency. As both organizations faced difficult changes that their life-stages required, they had strained the original informality to its limits. Based on the hopeful hypothesis that recognized the benefits and joys of mutual ministry, the conflict team encouraged Gayla to play more of an equal role to Geoff to balance his assumed senior status. She was to assume the full role of pastor of the church, with the authority granted to a pastor in the denomination's tradition. She was not to declare herself a power center, or to claim powers and privileges that were not rightly granted a pastor in a Protestant congregation, but she was to begin to play out her rightful role as director of worship, executive head of a small organization, and provider of pastoral services to the members of the congregation. Because she had the temporary role as interim pastor and because she was female, these efforts required extra diplomacy on her part, and they were received with mixed responses from both the congregation and from her colleague, Geoff Abbott. She persisted in playing her role, however, with a kind of innocent confidence that suggested she was only doing what she had been taught to do in seminary and what had been her practice in ministry in other churches prior to coming to Mission. This slight change in role set in motion other changes, including some new energizing of the church board, and more overt challenges to Geoff's informal power. While the relationship with Geoff remained cordial, there were underlying tensions that eventually boiled over into new conflict.

Continuing Structural Problems. The next issue in the realignment of structures at Mission Church arose when Geoff announced that he was performing the wedding of the daughter of a prominent member of Mission Church. The usual protocols in such matters required the family to approach the incumbent pastor to schedule a wedding, particularly if one wanted the pastor to invite someone else to officiate. While Gayla did not feel personally hurt that the family and Geoff had breached the protocols, she was concerned that the role of the pastor of the church was compromised when the director of BOM took over leadership in significant pastoral rituals such as weddings, funerals, and baptisms. In consultation with the conflict team, she initiated a conversation with Geoff in which she reminded him of the protocols, indicated that her concern was for the authority of the pastoral role, not for her own benefit, and asked him to deflect future requests from church members to her rather than simply assuming that he could officiate at weddings, funerals, and baptisms. This proved problematic. Geoff was offended at the suggestion that he would not have open access to play a pastoral role with members of the church, but angrily agreed to her request. He subsequently told key leaders in the congregation of this change in church practice, and as he intended, they responded with anger as well. Both Geoff's and the leaders' responses confirmed the hypothesis that they intended to hold on to the familiar ways of functioning rather than face the necessity to adapt to the changing needs of both the church and the agency.

Challenging the church and agency structures proved to be an exercise in frustration for both the conflict team and the members of the church board. Nothing in the reactions suggested that the hypothesis was incorrect, however, so the team moved on to the next levels of intervention.

Challenging the Stories

The Mission congregation believed in the story that they were a cutting-edge, mission-oriented, close-knit, and loving congregation. They continued to hold the image of themselves created during the time Jerry Brown and Jerry Garrison initiated the partnership between the congregation and the service organization. The church's name bore witness to its identity, even though the name was borrowed from the municipality in which the church was located. The City of Mission was named for the Jesuit church and hospital that preceded the settlement of the area before the area became part of the United States. The name of the community service agency also had its genesis in an earlier era, the late 1960s, when male language intended to refer to all human beings was still considered appropriate. The congregation liked to think that BOM was carrying out the church's mission of service to its neighbors. BOM considered its mission to be a secular social service, not particularly linked to Christian morals or beliefs.

Gathering Stories. Rather than directly challenge the identity issues, the conflict team and Gayla began their narrative interventions by simply gathering stories. Gayla led the church in congregational gatherings after church on two successive Sundays. On the first Sunday, she distributed large index cards and felt-tip markers, and asked everyone to think of their memories of key events in the life of the congregation. Since the church was less than forty years old, many of the original members were still active and present for these events. They then clustered in small groups to share the stories and clarify them. The following Sunday, she and the creative worship committee chairperson had prepared a large paper time chart on the walls around the all-purpose room of the church, marked in sections representing the decades of the church's history, with concurrent world, national, and local events pre-printed on the chart as a context for the church's story. She invited members to bring their cards forward, tell the story or describe the event they were remembering, and tape the cards on the paper chart to create a historical timeline. When everyone had placed their memory cards on the chart, she then reviewed it and asked if there were any gaps or inaccuracies in what had been reported so far. There was a lot of pride and energy reflected in the room that day as people remembered the early years of the church and the life of the congregation before the founding of BOM. One member remembered how BOM had begun in a coffee shop as the "Two Jerries" invented the idea of a way to serve the needs of the community. That whole program and its organizational functions had been outlined on paper napkins, to be implemented by the two friends in the life of the church. Only passing mention was given that day to Frank Braddock and his brief time as their pastor. Yet Gayla encouraged them to consider his time with them to have been as important a part of their story as any others, and she asserted that remembering it could enrich their sense of the church's story rather than threaten it. Someone mentioned the vote that ended Frank's ministry. A congregational meeting had been called to consider his resignation and the congregation had voted to accept his resignation, but the margin of decision was only four votes. Almost half of the congregation did not want Frank to leave and voted their desires. Remembering that part of their story in that moment served to challenge the congregation's self-identity as "one big happy family." But challenging the generally accepted story did not have to end with a hopeless story. Gayla suggested that, while the congregation had differences among them, their division represented more than just a fight over a particular minister. It was also about how the congregation was responding to the stresses of change in their personal lives, in the church, and in the world. On the Sundays that followed the two meetings, other members were invited to place their own stories and memories on the timeline, and the chart remained on the walls for several more weeks, prompting further reflection on the church's narrative.

Creating an Archetypal Story. Another way to challenge the story the church tells about itself is to introduce to the congregation an overarching story that catches the personality or character of the church. Just as the apostle on the Isle of Patmos described churches he knew with a particular kind of "angel" (Revelation 2–3), the character of a church can be given new hope and encouragement by telling parallel stories that members will recognize as close to their own. While biblical stories have significant interpretive power, they hold a special place in the hearts of members and don't readily hold as much metaphorical or archetypal power to evoke hope in transformation. Legends, myths, and literary stories that have archetypal significance can offer new inspiration in times of conflict.[2]

The conflict team grappled with this concept briefly and found themselves unable to identify a classical myth or literary story that adequately captured the angel of Mission Church. (This may be because the team had not reflected enough about the narrative elements of the congregation's life.) However, Gayla found herself

---

2. James Hopewell, *Congregation: Stories and Structures* (Minneapolis: Fortress, 1986), 113.

returning time and again in her sermons to the Lake Wobegon stories of the host of the public radio variety show *Prairie Home Companion*. Garrison Keillor's tales are often told from the same kind of ironic perspective that characterized the worldview of most of the members at Mission Church. They combine a delightful humor with a deeper sense that the people of Keillor's fictitious (if not mythical) hometown are flawed but funny human beings who struggle with the ordinary issues of their lives. Things don't always turn out the way they want or expect, but in many of the stories, the characters find their inner wisdom and strength to take care of each other and overcome the troubles of their lives. Stories like the Lutheran Pastors' retreat group that went out onto the lake on a pontoon boat that was not big enough for all of them, leaving them all waist-deep in lake water, challenge the mistaken identity of a group of people that they're all "above average." Everyone has their foibles, and the truth of living, from the ironic perspective, is to see the humor and find the goodness in the ordinariness of our lives. The members of Mission Church frequently commented on how much they appreciated Gayla's use of these stories in her sermons. She was, in fact, trying to find a way to challenge the "given" story by introducing an alternate, reconstructed story, basically in harmony with the worldview of the church, that held out hope and strength for a congregation, affirming them as they were.

Challenging the Symptoms

The conflict team and the interim pastor continued to encounter difficulties with the situation at Mission Church after the structural and narrative interventions just described. Tensions had increased between Geoff Abbott and Gayla, and members of the congregation had become more involved in unhealthy triangles, taking sides between the two. Suggestions to clarify and codify the structural arrangements between the church and BOM had prompted people to charge Gayla with trying to "ruin a good thing." The congregation appeared to have transferred their anxieties to Gayla and they were taking sides for either Gayla or Geoff. The church board was again finding it difficult to make clear decisions.

When structural and narrative interventions either have little effect or increase the tensions, a leader checks the hypothesis to see how the new information can inform and amend. In this situation, the responses and reactions appeared to confirm that the hypothesis was largely correct, but that the preferences for holding on to the old patterns were stronger than their interest in healthy adaptation, and the turbulence was increasing as changes continued to be needed.

The next action steps in such a situation are to challenge the symptoms of the frustration and turbulence. Four strategies are common in challenging the symptoms in conflicted churches — naming the underlying process issues, interrupting the symptoms, exploring the symptoms at different levels, and prescribing the symptom.

Naming the Underlying Process Issues. The team began its symptom interventions by having a meeting with the church board of Mission Church in which they discussed the difficulties entailed with a growing social service agency taking an increasingly larger role in the life of the two parallel institutions. Although the board was not ready to accept this as a concern, they did listen carefully to the analogy the team offered of the young adult who had grown up, begun a business, taken on a family, and yet was still living at home. Naturally the parents loved their adult offspring and wanted to be helpful. They also got a lot of pleasure from participating in the activities of the family and the business. Nonetheless, the parents were beginning to feel the strain of the extra challenges. Their own marriage, they began to realize, was being threatened by the presence of such a demanding entity as their child and both his family and his business in their home. The parents realized that they had helped to incubate this young adult's new life and had provided the space and energy and resources to make a success, but that neither they nor their adult child were flourishing in the current arrangement. Tearfully, and a bit fearfully, they began to suggest that it was time for the two families and the business to go their own ways. It was the parents' responsibility, the team suggested, to make the first move, thinking that the young adult may be both too comfortable in the old home setting and also too afraid about hurting the parents' feelings to move on. Many members of the board heard this story as applying to their own lives and their own ability to cut the apron strings for their own children, but did not quite see the application to Mission Church and BOM. Others saw it and resisted its truth. The team only asked that the board think about the story. They did not need to agree with it or take any particular action. In stating the suggestion that way, the team was able to introduce the metaphor for the issues behind the symptoms as if sowing a seed for later germination.

Interrupting the Symptoms. Interpreting the conflict with Frank Braddock as a symptom of the pervasive transformation under way in Mission Church and BOM the team asked Gayla to continue to raise questions about the structures and meaning of the relationship between the church and BOM. Although the team was hoping for a direct structural improvement, what actually happened was that the pattern of projecting problems onto Frank Braddock (making him the identified problem person) was interrupted. The system shifted its attention from Frank to Gayla and attempted to triangle her into the identified problem role. Congregation members reacted with anger and criticism toward her in several ways. When she and the team recognized this as a symptom of the resistance to change, they decided to go with that new interaction. The team coached Gayla on how to stay in relationship with the folks who were criticizing her while staying the course with her position. (This strategy is described more fully in the next chapter.) The informal term for what they asked her to do is to play "rope-a-dope." The term comes from a boxing strategy of Muhammad Ali in which he allowed his opponent to back him up to the ropes and pummel him with blows. Ali's strength and power allowed him to bounce off the ropes and withstand the blows while the opponent was worn down. By receiving the anger and the criticism and responding without attacking, defending, or explaining, the interaction failed to escalate the conflict as it had with Rev. Braddock, and so the symptom was interrupted.

Receiving such reactive anger cost Gayla the price of personal suffering because she had come to care about these people and it truly hurt her to have them turn against her. Because she had the full support and encouragement of the conflict team in the process, and because she also believed her staying steady and not reacting would be good for the congregation in the long run, she was able to keep her composure most of the time and provide good leadership for the church. Any time one part of the system is able to hold steady as the system tries out its worst symptoms, the system itself has to shift to find other ways to work out its anxieties about change. Looking past the crisis time, it is worth noting that the pastor who followed Gayla found himself able to make a successful ministry there without a significant reemergence of the old symptoms. Out of gratitude he sought out Gayla to specifically thank her for suffering for his sake. He understood the difficulty of the role she had taken on.

Exploring Issues at Different System Levels. As the symptoms continued at Mission Church, the team also considered other symptom interventions. An old family therapy strategy is to draw in other generations of the family to help address the anxieties. Such a cross-generational strategy can be adapted to a congregation by looking either to previous leaders (an earlier generation) of the congregation, or to involved supersystems or subsystems in the situation. Three of these were employed at Mission Church:

* *Cross-generational Strategy:* Inviting Jerry Brown back. The team suggested that the board and Gayla invite former pastor Jerry Brown back to the church for a commemorative event, asking him to preach and hoping his presence would offer a blessing to the congregation and its present situation. The hope was that such an event might release some of the energy being devoted to loyalty to the "old ways" of doing things. The invitation was duly made and Brown, for reasons never acknowledged, declined the invitation.

* *Working with a Supersystem:* Invoking the authority of the judicatory. After the earlier conversation with Geoff Abbott, in

which he agreed to avoid performing pastoral rituals for Mission Church members, Gayla learned that Geoff had agreed to another wedding of a prominent family of the church. At that point, the conflict team invoked the authority of the denominational rules to hold the church board accountable for this kind of boundary violation on Geoff's part. Although the board was angry and hurt that they had been "called on the carpet," they passed a resolution clearly setting forth the policies of the board regarding the pastor's role as the primary celebrant in congregational rituals such as weddings, funerals, and baptisms. This resolution, as a leadership role of the board (rather than one individual), did put a stop to the practice of members going directly to Geoff for their pastoral needs.

• *Working with Subsystems:* As Gayla made her rounds of pastoral care, she discovered that several of the families of key leaders of Mission Church were themselves in transitional crises of one kind or another. Several had adult children still living at home. Others were facing financial difficulties, dealing with problems with substance abuse, or experiencing marital problems. Being aware of the anxieties in these subsystems of the church, Gayla was able to use her counseling skills to guide families who were open to her help and to refer others to appropriate resources to find health and wholeness. The reduction in turmoil in key families played a role in reducing turmoil in the congregation as a whole.

Paradoxical Interventions. When a system is so enmeshed in its symptomatic behavior that it continues to resist direct, positive suggestions for better health, a reversal of suggestions can sometimes get to the deeper issues involved. Family therapists often refer to "prescribing the symptom"[3] as a way to move a family out of a stuck place. This is popularly called "reverse psychology": here, a leader suggests that the system (either a family or a congregation) go ahead and do what is causing it so much pain, even though that

---

3. Lynn Hoffman, *Foundations of Family Therapy: A Conceptual Framework for Systems Change* (New York: Basic Books, 1981), 19.

goes against the actual hopes for the situation. In the example of Mission Church, this took the form of encouraging a church fight. When the anger and criticism rose to noticeable levels, the team would suggest to the church board that they needed to hold another congregational forum after worship to give the congregation an opportunity to air their grievances. Guidelines for the fight were advertised in advance (see "Example of Ground Rules for Addressing Conflict" on page 33 above) and the church board members would be present and up front to receive and respond to any question or concern the members wished to bring. Three of these were held during the eighteen months of the interim time, and the levels of expressed anger and complaint were appreciably less than the earlier meetings held during the congregation's fight with Rev. Braddock. The reversal worked because when the team encouraged the church to fight, the church resisted the team's suggestion and paradoxically took a step toward health.

With this conflict utilization model, you don't need to take too seriously the emotional intensity of the conflict or the threats to the life of the congregation. It is more important to look beyond the presenting issues, to find the hopeful functions that these conflicts serve for the congregation, and to try a number of strategies that challenge the congregation to transcend their difficulties to find God's transforming power in and through the conflict. As the Mission Church case shows, this kind of initiative can play a profound role in the life of a congregation. I commend it to you as you cultivate in yourself a healthy perspective, prayerful clarity, decisiveness, and courage.

The Hope in Conflict Worksheet

To conclude this chapter, I introduce the Hope in Conflict Worksheet (see the followng page). This is a chart to help members, leaders, or outside consultants to pull together their observations and reflections and to plan strategies for turning conflict into creative transformation for their congregations as shown in the detail entered on the chart from Mission Church.

HOPE IN CONFLICT WORKSHEET FOR MISSION CHURCH

	Observations	Hypothesis	Action/Strategy	Progress
Structures	▪ Informal boundaries ▪ Unclear roles ▪ Encroachment of BOM	Single hypothesis, abbreviated in this column:	▪ Encourage more formality in mtgs. ▪ Naming—collaborative not mutual ▪ Mapping ▪ Reinforcing healthy structures ▪ Balancing power	Structural challenges increased tensions and increased symptoms
Stories	▪ "Mission" name/history ▪ "One big happy family" ▪ Jerry never left ▪ "2 Jerries" invented BOM	▪ Church and BOM in transition ▪ Neither can thrive in current crowded context ▪ Conflict in service to loyalty to old ideals and people ▪ New forms needed for both to thrive	▪ Historical timeline ▪ Challenging silence about Braddock ▪ Keillor as archetype of ironic goodness	Stories began to shift in reflecting on narratives
Symptoms	▪ Frank Braddock as identified problem ▪ Split vote to oust Frank ▪ Geoff taking weddings ▪ Angry reactivity to Gayla ▪ Families in crisis/transition ▪ Conflict instead of change		▪ Naming process—young adult story ▪ Interrupting—rope-a-dope ▪ Inviting Jerry back ▪ Invoking denom. power ▪ Strengthening families ▪ Prescribing church fights	▪ Good listening from leaders ▪ Stopped escalating anger ▪ Jerry declined ▪ Board acted appropriately to its power ▪ Families got better ▪ Flight to health

Reflection on
Challenging the System

1. Look again at your hopeful hypothesis and consider loving ways to challenge the system.

2. Identify at least one challenge each to the structures, the stories, and the symptoms of your situation.

3. Write a phrase or sentence that would describe how you would know if each challenge helped to move the congregation toward greater health.

Chapter Eight

Tapping the Leader's "Inner Sage"

My child, when you come to serve the Holy One, prepare yourself for testing. Set your heart right and be steadfast, and do not be impetuous in time of calamity. Cling to God and do not depart, so that your last days may be prosperous. . . . Those who are patient stay calm until the right moment, and then cheerfulness comes back to them. They hold back their words until the right moment; the lips of many tell of their good sense.
—Wisdom of Jesus ben Sirach, 2:1–4; 1:23–24

Dennis Clark had no idea he was serving as pastor of a conflicted congregation until he received a phone call from his denomination's regional minister asking for a lunch date. When he was told that two of his lay leaders had gone to the district office to ask for help in getting rid of their pastor, he was shocked and angry, and was ready to have lunch as soon as possible. Dennis knew that he was very different from his predecessor, the revered Pastor Bob, but he enjoyed the freedom the Middletown congregation gave him to be involved with youth ministry and to be a volunteer firefighter. He had made good friends among members of his congregation and was respected and appreciated among his colleagues in the city.

Recently, however, the personnel committee had been meeting without his knowledge and had established a set of criteria by which to judge their pastor's suitability for the congregation. The main theme on their list was that they wanted to be able to boast among their friends at other congregations that their pastor was a dynamic preacher and Bible teacher.

Dennis had been aware that people had been more critical lately and knew as a result that he had become less and less able to prepare a good sermon for Sunday mornings. He spent more time with the youth groups and less time in his study. Nonetheless, it was clear to him and to his regional minister that Dennis had done nothing that would merit losing his job.

From Pastor Clark's perspective, this appeared to be a conflict that was his either to win or to lose. He could fight his opponents and prove his worth as their pastor or admit defeat and resign. The regional minister, however, invited Dennis to take a more hopeful view of his situation and move it beyond his personal stakes of winning or losing. He did not have to accept the role of "identified problem" that the conflicted factions of his church had projected onto him. Instead he could choose to be a wise leader, attending to the structures, stories, and symptoms of the situation, and keep a healthy sense of himself.

Finding Hope in Middletown

Sooner or later as a leader you face the push and pull of a congregation that expects too much and criticizes every disappointed expectation. As I have defined leadership in earlier chapters, we each need to learn to combine faithfulness to our own integrity with respectfulness in our community with the people with whom we share a congregational life. The model of conflict utilization described in the previous chapters is best handled by someone willing to grow into maturity and become wise in the ways of the church. If I did not believe that such maturity and wisdom were possible, I would not have written this book. Follow our colleague Dennis Clark as he grapples with his own crisis of wisdom and maturity.

With the help of the regional minister, Dennis began to see his situation from a more hopeful frame of reference. He recognized that those who "have the problem," represented by the leaders who brought the complaint, had projected all the church's problems onto him. Apparently the tension had risen to such high levels of discomfort among the members that they had adopted what seemed to them to be the simple solution: to eliminate him as their pastor. They naively assumed that by getting rid of him all their problems would be solved.

On careful reflection Pastor Clark began to see his situation more clearly and calmly. The "problem" defined by his critics was that there was a poor match between the congregation and the pastor. But a more hopeful perspective helped him to recognize that the dislocation lay in his congregation, which was split between what he called a "country club" group, who saw their church as comfortable, sociable, fun, and not very demanding, and the "adventurous" group, who expected their church to be a source of excitement and challenge.

It was the "adventurers" who had played the major role in the search committee that called Dennis, and, imagining that this group represented the spirit of the whole congregation, he had happily accepted their invitation to lead them to serve in the community. After Dennis was installed, the "adventurers" assumed their work was done, and the majority membership on the church board reverted back to the "country club" group. The problem appeared to belong to these two groups, who were at odds with each other but unwilling to address the differences in their views about church. This is not unlike parents who project their marital tensions on a particular child instead of working on their marriage. These competing factions in the church played off each other with the pastor in the middle, and the conflict was the apparent symptom of that triangle.

When did this problem begin? It began when the "country-club" group regained leadership on the governing board of the Middletown church and one of their group became chair of the personnel committee. As these "country-club" church members recognized that Dennis was not exactly what they had expected him to be, the old-time leaders decided to apply their simple solution, and the two groups found that they suddenly had something they could agree on when they focused on the pastor as the problem.

Dennis also became more aware that he had accepted the role of identified problem and, without realizing it, was protecting his congregation from splitting in half by acting out their projections with his angry opposition to their demands. At that point, Dennis realized that he had a different reason for seeking help. He asked the regional minister to explore with him the possibility of some solution other than terminating his pastoral relationship.

From a larger perspective Dennis was able to reduce his anger and reactivity and seek assistance in choosing a different role. At that point, the regional minister began to coach Dennis in the understanding of wise and mature leadership.

The Practice of Wise, Mature Church Leadership

As a leader in the midst of congregational conflict, you can take encouragement from the fact that, although you may not be able to change the entire system singlehandedly, you can help the congregation become healthier by becoming healthier yourself. This idea of the self-differentiated leader has gained acceptance in the past decade. It is a concept that is potentially transformative for individuals and for systems, but it is not an easy one to describe. The model that follows has evolved over the years in my personal experience and teaching and has been nurtured by theological reflection into a description of mature wisdom.

The term "wisdom" comes from a study of the sages of the Bible.[1] When we have looked to the Bible for leadership models, we have often focused on the four roles of leadership in the Hebrew Scriptures:

+ prophets — called in crisis to see and proclaim where the people have gone astray,

+ monarchs — anointed to godly governance,

---

1. I was introduced to the idea of wisdom in connection with self-differentiation in the work of Ronald W. Richardson, *Creating a Healthier Church* (Minneapolis: Fortress Press, 1996), chapter 6, 80ff. The work of Donn Morgan, *The Making of Sages: Biblical Wisdom and Contemporary Culture* (Harrisburg, PA: Trinity Press International, 2002), offers a thorough look at the sages. The addition of the term "maturity" comes from Frank A. Thomas, *Spiritual Maturity: Preserving Congregational Health and Balance* (Minneapolis: Fortress, 2002).

+ priests — authorized to mediate the presence and forgiveness of God in worship, and

+ rabbis — trained to teach the torah, to interpret the laws of God in the lives of the people.

But we have ignored another very important role, that of the sages, who were gifted with wise discernment to guide family and community in dreaming and interpreting dreams. The sages are celebrated in the wisdom literature, and in several key leaders. That Joseph and Daniel were shown serving as sages in foreign courts, discerning the meaning of dreams and events, shows that the role was known and accepted in Israel. Both men and women served as sages, and the wisdom literature typically refers to the female form of wisdom, Sophia. Esther, Deborah, and Abigail are among the named biblical women who served their community by offering wise counsel and discernment.

Sages are those whom Brueggemann calls the practical theologians of the Bible.[2] They were not institutionalized, not usually installed in one of the ordained roles. They were advisors to families and the whole community. Sages drew from the order and demands of God's creation (systems, process), recognized the enigmas and dailyness of life (an ironic worldview), and knew God through deep mystical experiences, often beyond and beneath the law and the temple. The wisdom of the sages provides a helpful model for leading in the midst of conflict in a congregation by understanding how the world works and how a deeper mystery informs the leader's path.

Learning from the wisdom tradition, I call leaders to tap their own inner sages by focusing on two different kinds of ability. One set of abilities focuses on the freedom of the self as given by God. The matching set of abilities points to communion among human beings and between humans and the divine. The theological foundation for this model is the process theology of Daniel Day

---

2. Walter Brueggemann, *Theology of the Old Testament* (Minneapolis: Fortress, 1997), 685.

Williams.[3] Williams identifies the structures of love that are found in the design of the fabric of existence. Both the human experience of love and God's love are structured around the interplay of freedom and communion.

FREEDOM AND COMMUNION
AS WISE, MATURE LEADERSHIP

Abilities of a Leader as a Wise Self with Freedom and Integrity

1. Achieves clarity in discerning her own life goals and values.

2. Takes responsibility for his own actions, feelings, and well-being.

3. Tolerates and makes constructive use of her own suffering.

4. Regulates his own reactivity.

Abilities of a Leader as a Wise Self in Communion

5. Stays in relationships in the system.

6. Accepts that others are free individuals who are responsible for their own actions, feelings, and well-being.

7. Allows others to experience suffering as a consequence of their own behavior.

8. Keeps a hopeful perspective.

---

3. Daniel Day Williams, *The Spirit and the Forms of Love* (New York: Harper & Row, 1968).

Abilities of a Leader as a Wise Self with Freedom and Integrity

1. Achieves Clarity in Discerning Her Own Life Goals and Values

Built into the design for human life is the freedom of each of us to choose personal life goals and values. When our friends ask us for help with a decision they are making, and most of what they are worrying about is what others will think if they make one choice or another, we do well to encourage them to be clear first about what they want and how that fits into their personal goals and values as individuals. Of course what others think is important information, and the commitments we have made to others limit our freedom. But concern for what others think cannot replace clarity about one's self. Congregations exert pressures to act or not act in particular ways, and the wise leader has to choose between the outside pressure and the internal integrity of the self. Dennis Clark recognized his basic goal was to continue to be the pastor in Middletown. At the same time, he was aware of his deeper value, which was to help his people grasp the need to speak and act to bring peace and justice to the world around them. Defining his goal and value helped him to find his freedom. He realized he needed to be able to choose whether he wanted to hold on to his goal, or whether he would put his passion for justice on the back burner in order to stay on as the pastor of his church. Through prayer, reflection, and personal discernment, Dennis learned to define who he was, what he believed, and what he was called to do in the particular situation.

2. Takes Responsibility for His Own Actions, Feelings, and Well-Being

With a sense of clarity comes the second ability: to take responsibility for one's own actions, feelings, and well-being. When a leader chooses the role of victim or reactor in a conflict situation, the most common rationale for that choice is that someone else "made me" act or feel that way or even made me not take care of myself. The

⌐re leader learns to avoid that rationalization and to recognize that no one else is responsible for what one does. Feelings,
too, can be said to originate from the thinking process of the individual. When a person interprets a scene or words, and then reacts
with emotion, it is the person's own interpretation that is responsible for the emotion. That's why careful systems thinking about the
situation or about others helps one to be responsible for one's own
feelings. Regarding well-being, we have others around us who care
about us, including our parents, spouses, partners, children, friends,
and other church members. But they are not primarily responsible
for our well-being. Some people, and especially some pastors, assume that the church always looks out for the pastor's well-being,
but as the case of Dennis Clark indicates, this assumption does not
always hold true. Especially in time of conflict, a leader needs to be
accountable to her or his own self for self-care. As the second set
of abilities will show, this does not eliminate the compassion and
involvement the leader has with others in the system.

A simple aphorism I learned from family systems theory helps
check on the level of self-responsibility in the face of anxiety and
conflict: "Don't attack, don't defend, and don't explain." Wise,
mature leaders learn to make clear statements about themselves,
about what they have done or will do, about how they feel, and
about what they want and need. Such clear statements work better than attacks on others, which focus on alleged defects in others
rather than on the leader's own responsibility. Whenever leaders are
tempted to defend themselves or even to explain their actions, they
have relegated to others the responsibility to judge them, instead
of relying on their own integrity. Instead of attacking, defending,
or explaining, they prefer to let their word be " 'Yes, Yes' or 'No,
No' " (Matthew 5:37).

3. Tolerates and Makes Constructive Use of Her Own Suffering

Whenever we assert our freedom and take responsibility for ourselves, and for that matter whenever we love someone, we make
ourselves vulnerable to rejection and sorrow. Although Western

culture has often failed to recognize it, suffering is a part of love. The wise, mature leader is able to tolerate and make constructive use of his or her own suffering. One pastor has written of church leadership in times of trouble: "One's ability to tolerate and handle one's own pain constructively is the key to avoiding the posture of victim."[4]

By contrast, in one's foolishness or immaturity, one may try to avoid pain and suffering by trying reactive or protective stances. Experience shows that avoiding or delaying pain usually brings more suffering later. In the example of Dennis Clark, he at first attempted to avoid feeling his own pain by lashing out at his critics. As he stepped back from his immediate reaction, however, he gradually became able to face the criticism and acknowledge the pain he felt at their rejection of him and his pastoral leadership. This experience was simultaneously painful and constructive. The pain of rejection evoked all of the personal fears and doubts that were part of his personality. He also discovered that he did not have to be a victim to the power plays of others. He was strong enough to face the pain of their disapproval and turn his fear and self-doubt into opportunities to grow and develop as a better leader and a better human being. If one desires to love the people and the church as a whole when conflict erupts, one does well to face and experience the pain, moving through it and learning from it, rather than avoiding it.

4. Regulates His Own Reactivity

Perhaps you already know the term "non-anxious presence" used in talking about self-differentiation.[5] The term was used by some family therapy writers to encourage persons to find a way to be healthy in an anxious system. In response to that concept, many church leaders have become more anxious because they want to be "non-anxious" in the presence of their church systems, but find they are unable to erase their own anxiety. In response I have taught "there's no such thing as a non-anxious presence." If you are really

---

4. Frank A. Thomas, *Spiritual Maturity: Preserving Congregational Health and Balance* (Minneapolis: Fortress, 2002), 94.

5. Edwin Friedman, *Generation to Generation* (New York: Guilford, 1985).

a leader of a system, and that system is anxious, then you will feel the anxiety.

The task for the wise, mature leader is to avoid letting the anxiety of the system derail the leader's own freedom and integrity. Dennis Clark had identified with his congregation so much that he could not separate himself emotionally from the emotions and criticisms of its members. He was being reactive. His regional minister was able to help him regulate his reactivity, another phrase that better fits the reality of leadership in emotional systems. The word "regulate" suggests the ability to make adjustments in something to return it to a desired level of functioning. "Reactivity" refers to the extent to which a person engages in a situation without reflecting or exercising full freedom and integrity.

In the heat of the conflict, Dennis Clark experienced several of the most common patterns of reactivity.[6] At first, Dennis was tempted to react with *compliance* by caving in to the emotional demands of his anxious members to be their ideal pastor. His reactive alternative was *rebellion* by becoming an even worse preacher than they accused him of being. When he wanted to reply to the situation by asking his supporters to help him "win" the conflict, he was demonstrating the reactivity pattern of *power struggles.* Later when all he wanted to do was to resign, he was reacting by *emotional distancing.* He discovered, however, that regulating reactivity did not require heroic measures of calm response. By recognizing that the messages were not simply "about what was wrong with him," but were outcroppings of the fears and conflicts built into the congregation's story, Dennis was able to ratchet down his reactivity. That slight adjustment went a long way in shifting the tone of the whole system.

In regulating reactivity, Dennis was also learning to balance emotion and reason in choosing responses to a situation. He was employing what Daniel Day Williams called "impartial judgment in loving concern for the other."[7] When Dennis stopped to reflect on his response, he was loving his congregation by seeking

---

6. Richardson, *Creating a Healthier Church,* chapter 7.
7. Williams, *The Spirit and the Forms of Love,* 121.

a more objective perspective on the truth in both himself and in the members of the church. His choice to regulate his reactivity demonstrated what Williams called "the high tribute which love pays to the other, the tribute of seeking the truth in the other and the other in the truth."[8] This rationality does not negate the role of emotion in human relationships, nor does it promote what some would call an overly masculine perspective. It simply calls the leader to a more exacting standard of loving that appreciates both thinking and emotion as important elements of the human being.

Striving to be both clear and responsible for one's own actions and feelings and well-being, a wise leader learns to think carefully before reacting, to ask questions before lashing out, and to seek to understand impartially both herself and the other before assigning blame.

Without a sense of self, leadership does not become wise or mature. However, the self alone does not describe a wise, mature leader. A sense of connection with the community, with the people God has given, is the companion to a sense of self.

Abilities of a Leader as a Wise Self in Communion

5. Stays in Relationships in the System

You can see that the abilities to be clear and responsible and relatively calm in oneself, taken by themselves, seem to be fairly accessible. When you are also expected to be interacting with others on a regular basis during a conflict, then you'll find clarity, responsibility, and calmness harder to achieve. To grow into wise, mature leadership, you will want to follow Harriet Lerner's advice and "hang in, stay out, and stay calm."[9] By that she meant to "hang in" with the difficult relationships while staying out of unhealthy triangles in a calm manner. This advice sounds contrary to common sense in the face of angry criticism or hurtful opposition. Dennis Clark, for example,

---

8. Ibid.
9. Harriet G. Lerner, *The Dance of Anger* (New York: Harper and Row, 1985), 183.

spent a lot of energy in the weeks that followed his conversation with the regional minister avoiding the people who were his worst critics. He could not bear to face them and was afraid his anger would erupt or that they would find even more to criticize as a result. He was advised to work at staying in touch. Instead of distancing from his critics, he began a program of intentionally making calls on those most antagonistic to him. He was able to do this by changing the premise for these contacts from being "sociable," which was the way his congregation defined their usual relations with their pastor, to being "pastoral," meaning playing the official role of the position he held. He would discuss church business with them, inquire as to their family's health and well-being, invite comments about his latest sermons without getting defensive about it, have a prayer with them, and take his leave. As he did, he discovered a new confidence rising in himself, and his businesslike approach to his critics blunted their desire to blame everything on him. Staying in relationship does not necessarily result in easier relationships, but it does make a difference in the overall tone of the whole system of relationships.

Staying in touch, as envisioned here, refers to a genuine presence with others in which one makes one's whole self available. Instead of being a threatening and potentially dangerous enterprise, however, staying in touch puts us at a more rewarding and deeper level of our humanity with each other. This deeper connection also brings with it an element of risk. In love we not only act, but we are acted upon by others, and their actions move us, limit us, and potentially transform us, but they never destroy our integrity and freedom.[10] Thus, whenever the wise, mature leader is tempted to pull away from a system in conflict, he or she can be encouraged to "hang in" by the Christian ethic of love.

6. Accepts That Others Are Free Individuals Who Are Responsible for Their Own Actions, Feelings, and Well-Being

As a mirror to the ability to take responsibility for one's own self, the second ability on the communion side is accepting that others are

---

10. Williams, *The Spirit and the Forms of Love*, 115.

responsible for their own selves. This is often a difficult concept for church leaders who take very seriously their responsibility to love and care for others. The key to this ability is found in the notion of human freedom. If I am to see myself as free and responsible for myself, I must recognize the freedom of others as well. This ability involves recognizing that adults are "grown up" and are usually at their best when they are treated as responsible, free adults. This is another element of Christian love[11] that cannot be commanded or coerced. This reflects the love of God that grants humans freedom to love God in return or to reject God's love.

In contrast to the freedom of God's love, the human tendency is to use a controlling kind of love. The lay leaders of the Middletown church tried to take away Dennis's freedom to be responsible for himself. They wanted to direct his actions and his feelings to benefit their own agenda. The conflict in that congregation was, in part, about the difficulty of that congregation to allow people — especially their pastor — the freedom to be different from the expectations the congregation had of them.

Of course, there are individuals who cannot take full responsibility for themselves, including children, the ill, and those whose abilities are otherwise impaired. We have a responsibility to carefully restrict their actions, guide their emotions, and watch out for their well-being to the extent that they cannot do so. Even such individuals need as much freedom as they can handle, and love requires encouraging them toward greater freedom to take their own responsibility.

7. Allows Others to Experience Suffering as a Consequence of Their Own Behavior

One of our biggest challenges in becoming wise, mature leaders is how to be sensitive to the pain and suffering of members of the church without taking responsibility for that suffering. The question, "Don't you care that the Angstroms are angry about the

---

11. Ibid., 116.

decision for the youth mission trip to go to an inner city neighbor-hood?" evokes the leader's savior responses: the leader is tempted to shift the church's decisions just a little bit to relieve the Angstroms' pain. The leader is tempted to accept responsibility for that pain and to rescue them from their anxiety. Of course, taking the path of least resistance to the Angstroms is likely to throw at least one other family and the staff members into deep suffering, for which the leader will also feel responsible. The cycle of playing savior to the suffering of others can be never-ending. But even more, the underlying problem with that cycle is a failure of responsibility and freedom. The Angstroms are responsible for themselves and are free to experience their pain and suffering as part of their Christian ex-perience. The leader has compassion for them but has to remember that taking responsibility for them takes away their freedom. Frank Thomas points to his experience as church leader of struggling with this particular issue.

> My pain lessens when I am able to accept that the other per-son is free to choose what is in his or her best interest, and my best choice is to accept that decision and live with it.... If we can accept and face the pain, learn from it, and accept the limits of life that it teaches, then we will grow and mature. If we constructively handle our pain, we will develop reason-able expectations of life that remove the apparent necessity of playing the role of victim or savior.[12]

The wise, mature leader is able to sort through the complexities of freedom and responsibility to avoid debilitating savior and vic-tim cycles for everyone concerned. Others may choose to pick up those roles if the leader does not, but the leader's first responsibility is to the position of leadership, not the behaviors of all the other members of the system.

---

12. Thomas, *Spiritual Maturity*, 25.

8. Keeps a Hopeful Perspective

The last ability on the communion side of the list serves as a helpful summary of the entire description of the wise, mature leader. You probably noticed that in conflict it is easy to lose a sense of perspective on the situation. When the content of the conflict is personally important to the you, perspective is even harder. Careful reflection and a hopeful outlook help you to relate to people in a more relaxed way. Perspective helps you to take yourself more lightly, less seriously in the pulls of stresses of the system. Perspective is defined here as the ability to stay in relationships without controlling or being controlled. Perspective is an antidote to overly serious attitudes and reactions. When anxiety is high in a human system, and tensions grow more and more uncomfortable, there is a tendency for the participants to get more serious about what is going on. Seriousness is often a desperate attempt on the part of the system as a whole to bring a situation back into older patterns of balance. Any member of a super-serious system who can relax and behave somewhat differently than is expected serves as a wise, mature leader.

This kind of perspective has been compared to playfulness in family therapy, because perspective sometimes allows a leader to find some humor in a situation or even to adopt a strategy that goes in the opposite direction of one's usual or intuitive responses. For example, when a colleague who is working too hard wonders out loud if she should take some time off, a playful response might be to say, "Oh, for heaven's sake, don't go to that kind of extreme!" Instead of buying into a win-lose attitude about a situation, perspective allows a person to drop back and see a longer or larger view and to value the relationships and the love more than the outcome of the particular issue at hand. It has been compared with two ways of playing games.[13] A short-range or finite perspective prompts us to play games that end in winning and losing and that are played with seriousness. A longer range or infinite perspective allows people to

---

13. James Carse, *Finite and Infinite Games: A Vision of Life as Play and Possibility* (New York: Ballantine, 1986).

pursue a game with playfulness because their purpose is continuing to play, continuing to be in relationship with other players.

To hold an infinite perspective in churches is to affirm others while refusing to be controlled by their emotions. When a church matriarch asked a young pastor's wife for some information about a future program of the church, the pastor's wife stated that she did not know. The matriarch put more pressure on the young woman for the expected information. The pastor's wife asserted that she and her husband did not talk about church business when they were at home. "Well, what do you do?" demanded the matriarch. With a smile (and an infinite perspective) the younger woman said, "Why, we make love." Her perspective broke the seriousness of the interaction and made it possible for her and the matriarch to become good friends.

Perspective allows you as a wise, mature leader to choose from a greater variety of possible actions. For Dennis Clark it meant being less antagonistic toward the personnel committee. Eventually he was able to smile genuinely and tell the chair of the committee that it might be a good idea for them to have some more meetings without him because he was sure they had not come up with the worst stuff about his ministry. Perhaps, he suggested, they should interview his own teenage daughters, who were particularly good at criticizing their dad. He also began taking a lighter attitude toward his preaching. Whenever he found himself blocked by worry about what people would think about his next sermon, he simply imagined the sermon he was working on as his last sermon in that church, and he was always able to think of interesting and challenging things to write. Paradoxically, the conflict in the church began to diminish when Dennis was able to be less serious and more interested in relationships and truth than he was in meeting all the expectations of his antagonists.

These eight abilities of freedom and communion are a helpful foundation for building healthier relationships within a congregation. When church members want to blame others for what has gone wrong in their church, they are missing an opening for mercy, both for themselves and for others. When they accept their own role and responsibility through wise and mature leadership, they tap a resource of grace that can transform the worst of human situations.

Evaluating How You're Doing in the Middle of Conflict

In case you're wondering how you might be able to gauge your levels of self-differentiation at various points along the way, several family therapy leaders have offered some help. The chart on the following page brings together much of that research and conceptual work into eight scales of wise maturity in leadership. In addition to the eight abilities listed above, the chart includes concepts from Frank Thomas, who says that mature leadership is "the spiritual process of discerning what one believes (clarity), acting on that belief in the public arena (decisiveness), and standing behind that action despite the varied responses of people (courage)."[14] The scales also use the indicators of reactivity taken from Ronald Richardson: compliance, rebellion, power struggles, and emotional distancing.[15] In a given situation, use the chart to evaluate how you are doing with your anxiety and your wise maturity.

It helps to remember that this chart, and the eight abilities behind it, is only an indicator of what is happening inside the self at the moment a leader applies the scales. When the results show higher levels of anxiety and reactivity, be assured that no one is ever expected to be a perfect "1" all the time. The experts in family therapy tell us that we have to manage to be wise and mature only about 60 percent of the time in order to be effective. Murray Bowen wrote in 1972 of his own 100-point scale of self-differentiation that "it has not yet been possible to check the scale on extremely high-level people, but my impression is that 75 is a very high-level person and that those above 60 constitute a small percentage of society."[16] The

---

14. Thomas, *Spiritual Maturity*, 96.
15. Richardson, *Creating a Healthier Church*, chapter 7.
16. Murray Bowen, *Family Therapy in Clinical Practice* (Northvale, NJ: Jason Aronson, 1986), 474.

SCALES OF WISE MATURITY IN LEADERSHIP

Think of yourself in a particular situation in your life, either present or past, and rate your functioning by marking where you are on each of the following scales. The numbers indicate the amount of anxiety you are demonstrating as you relate to the system. The higher the score, the more reactive you are at the moment.

Acceptance of suffering	1	2	3	4	5	Victim or Savior
Clarity	1	2	3	4	5	Confusion
Decisiveness	1	2	3	4	5	Indecision
Courage	1	2	3	4	5	Anxiety
Integrity	1	2	3	4	5	Compliance
Communion	1	2	3	4	5	Rebellion
Trust the Process	1	2	3	4	5	Power Struggle
Participation	1	2	3	4	5	Distancing

effort is in remembering to keep these abilities in mind in the push and pull of congregational life.

In previous chapters I have described practical and concrete methods to hopefully assess a conflict in your congregation, and to identify strategies for challenging your congregation to tap its own resources of health and wholeness. In all of those methods and strategies, I have assumed your efforts to be present as a wise, mature, and hopeful leader to ask questions, sort out relational puzzles, and act strategically. It is the eight abilities of self-differentiated leadership that lay a foundation for a congregation to learn to define itself in healthier ways. I have known many cases in which a single individual — who was able to be clear in naming and re-framing the situation and also was able to stay connected when conflict raged in a congregation — could tap into the hopefulness of the system and help move relationships toward the changes that God was prompting. In some situations, unfortunately, no matter what a clear, connected, wise, and mature individual did, the conflict escalated into chaotic and destructive patterns, and the system and the people in it were disabled and efforts toward health were frustrated. Either way, the leader was responsible only for her or his own efforts and behavior and not for the final results of the interactions.

Reflection on Your Inner Sage

1. Take some quiet time and reflect in general on your own efforts to be a self-differentiated leader. In what areas have you grown toward wise maturity in recent times? In what areas would you like to practice to improve your ability?

2. Fill in the "scales of wise maturity" form. Quietly reflect on your scores. What surprised you? What areas of personal growth can you identify for yourself?

3. Identify partners who can assist you in growing to greater maturity and wisdom, especially as you face a conflict situation.

4. Take some quiet time and give yourself forgiveness for times when you have fallen short of the ideal of self-differentiation. Then give yourself permission to fall short again in the stresses of your life, only to reflect and learn and grow.

Chapter Nine

The Mystery of Conflict Unveiled

WHY THE THREE KEYS WORK

Everything that exists in this world has a heart, and that heart has a heart that is the heart of the world. According to [a] Sage, sound becomes voice, voice becomes song, and song becomes story. If only we lend an ear, we will hear what is all around us. The leaves of the trees speak to the grass, the clouds signal one another, and the wind carries secrets from one land to the next. One must learn to listen: that is the key to mystery.

— Elie Wiesel[1]

When you take a hard look at your congregation in conflict, you see that members resort to displays of anger and fear, interpersonal trust turns to distrust, issues give way to personalities, the debate turns to a win-lose context, facts are distorted, and individuals are singled out for attack. If the conflict is allowed to fester, cold self-righteousness and ideological fervor motivate members to try to get rid of their opponents.[2] In all this noisy confusion, you might be tempted to identify any one of these factors as "the problem" or "the cause." If you choose the way of the wise leader, you can learn to recognize that these are only the part of the situation that shows on the surface. While they are painfully real, they obscure the deeper, hidden ways the congregation is interconnected and the ways God is calling them to transformation.

---

1. Elie Wiesel, *The Time of the Uprooted* (New York: Alfred Knopf, 2005), 321.
2. Descriptive words from "When Conflict Erupts in Your Congregation: Interview with Speed Leas" in *Conflict Management in Congregations,* ed. David Lott (Bethesda, MD: Alban Institute, 2001), 16.

The Epistle to the Ephesians is a good scriptural foundation for finding hope in conflict. In Ephesians 3:4–5 Paul writes about the mystery of Christ that was hidden but is now revealed. The Greek word for mystery used there is *musterion,* whose root is *myein,* meaning to shut or close. "Mystery" is that which is hidden, or covered by ordinary experiences.

The mystery has been "revealed," which translates the Greek word *apokalupsis,* meaning to uncover or unveil.

The ways of God in the world and beyond the world are too full to be contained in any given experience or any given idea. They are mysterious.[3] Only prayerful, careful, observant discernment can see the slow unveiling of the truth.

The deeper, hidden wisdom and goodness of a congregation presents itself like the jumble of jigsaw puzzle pieces dumped out of the box onto the table. They have to be turned over and carefully arranged and rearranged to find the hidden picture or pattern. Some people begin by arranging the border pieces and then filling in the blanks. Others "solve" jigsaw puzzles by finding pieces that seem to go together and slowly find how like pieces reveal parts of the picture. An experienced jigsaw puzzle worker knows that no single piece nor groups of pieces will reveal the picture. Only after many parts and pieces are fitted and placed does the whole come into view.

Unveiling the Mysteries of Conflict

In each of the eight church conflicts discussed in the previous chapters, many difficulties crowded the surface of the situation, and in each case the deeper wisdom of hope and goodness was initially hidden. Using the three keys of structures, stories, and symptoms,

---

3. The use of the term "mystery" here is more metaphorical than absolutely precise. Paul Tillich, *Systematic Theology,* vol. 1 (Chicago: University of Chicago Press, 1951), 109, wants to limit the term to the full mystery of God, which is beyond ordinary cognitive investigation. In this book I refer both to the hidden inner truth about a congregation's life, which can be uncovered by this way of seeing, and the truly mysterious presence and working of God in, through, and beyond the particular situation.

we have seen how leaders were able to experience the "gradual unveiling of truth."[4] What follows is my interpretation of those hidden
truths, admittedly from the vantage point of looking backward.

◆ *The Church Key* (chapter 1). Our consultants were thoroughly
distracted by the red-herring issue of the key to the kitchen. A
natural desire for a quick fix to the difficulties led them to conclude that they had uncovered the truth of the situation, and
they left with the job only partly done. If they had looked at the
structures of the church, they might have seen a lack of clarity of
boundaries and roles and some power inequalities. More careful
listening to the stories might have unveiled the desperation the
leaders were feeling about the changes happening in their community and in their church. They might have learned that the
symptom of the conflict was not only about the hard feelings
over the locks on the kitchen doors, but also about feeling stuck
in a 1950s mode of being church in the 1970s world.

◆ *Antioch Church* (chapter 2). Neither the good lay leaders of Antioch Church, nor Pastor Joe Freeman, nor the church board
could get their minds around the congregation's emotions (or
their own), while the congregation was moving into more confusion and more broken relationships. This was an experience of a
congregation whose transformation had spun into chaos. Rather
than perceive the chaos as something bad or destructive, the denominational consultants were able to look beyond the surface
to the history, the culture, and the context of Antioch Church
to see God at work to bring the church to a transformation that
would begin a new pattern of life and mission.

◆ *Big Bluff City* (chapter 3). The regional minister Agnes and her
partner Bill were wise to look beneath the surface issue of Pastor
Percy Noble's job performance. They carefully noted and gra-
ciously declined to act on the symptoms of Percy's illness and the
reactivity of Annabelle's call for help. Instead they focused on the
most direct approach by looking at the structures of the church.

---

4. P. D. James, *The Lighthouse* (London: Faber and Faber, 2005), 10.

The willingness of both the pastor and the members of the church board to organize themselves in healthier ways, honoring order and accountability in the church's polity, made an elegant conclusion to what had been a big bluff of turbulence. In the process of the conflict consultation, the pastor and the church board members found hope for their story. They began to notice who were playing the roles of helper, reactor, and villain (characters in the narrative analysis of the church's story; see chapter 4) and they called them to account. On reflection, we saw that Annabelle was in fact more a helper than a troublemaking reactor because she was willing to call for outside help when no one else could take constructive, hopeful action.

♦ *Endwell Community* (chapter 4). Things did not look like they would end well for the Endwell congregation. In fact it took a few years to let the stories provide some healing hope for that situation. In a congregation with an experimental church structure, the power of stories took precedence. Both the leaders and the pastor were able to move from painful reaction and fearful attempts to control to a more faithful stance of interpreting the movement of God among them. Distressing signs of decline in membership and money had led to conflict because they needed to find a more positive, appreciative, and hopeful frame for the church's story as they moved into the next chapters of their lives.

♦ *Old Hickory* (chapter 5). Confronted with chaos that soon engulfed him, interim pastor Walt Lindsey was eventually able to see that his two staff colleagues were not just difficult but indeed had been chosen by the system to be the identified problems. He correctly interpreted the raging emotions and anxieties as symptoms of the deeper changes in and around the historic church. Using the three keys of structures, stories, and symptoms at Old Hickory led Walt to discover the public secret of past clergy sexual misconduct. The energy expended to protect that secret had kept the congregation from its natural ability to shift and adapt to the ordinary changes of its life. The series of crises built to an emotional peak that finally allowed an outside consultant to help the congregation learn from its symptoms and restore its flexibility and hope in the flow of change.

◆ *Ugly Duckling* (chapter 6). Suzanna Sennette might have presided over the demise of a congregation if she had taken the self-descriptions of her new congregation at face value. The surface story maintained that the previous pastor had ruined the congregation and that once loving members no longer could talk to each other. Instead, she wisely sorted through the pieces of the puzzle, allowing her imagination to pull together the larger picture. Neither the immediate former pastor nor his supporters and opponents were culprits. Instead of assigning blame, Sennette used a positive hypothesis to encourage the lay leaders to take back their own wisdom and strength and face the new challenges of their life together with faith. After a while, the graceful beauty of the congregation emerged for everyone to see.

◆ *Mission Community* (chapter 7). This church was in so much turmoil that it required the intentional intervention of the designated leader in collaboration with a team of outside leaders. The mystery of conflict in a self-described happy family began to make sense when the larger context of Mission Church was clearly seen. The intrusive demands of the social service agency (BOM) overshadowed and diminished the ability of the congregation to adapt to its changing circumstances. Power inequities between the BOM and the congregation were balanced by the intervention of the denominational team, and the separate identities of the church and its pastor were each also strengthened by it.

◆ *Middletown* (chapter 8). The story of Dennis Clark focused on the way a leader finds wisdom and hope in a conflict situation. The keys to the hidden hope in conflict are best if used by someone who is able both to maintain a sense of self as a free and integrated whole and to stay in communion with God and the interconnected living system of the congregation. In fact, part of the mystery of interconnected systems is that the influence of a single calm, loving, and hopeful person can make a positive difference in the whole system.

How the Keys Work

In each case the keys of structures, stories, and symptoms unlocked the hidden mystery behind the "presenting issues." These keys are not ultimate or absolute. They need to be practiced, improved, and adapted as needed to the growing awareness of truth in the church and in the world. Nonetheless, they do help leaders to clear their eyes and see, hear, and learn more about the mystery of God's people and God's work. Derived from a synthesis of social science theory (family systems), physical science theory (the new physics), and theological reflection (process and liberation theology), these keys work because they are tied to something that is true and deep about the world.

Structures Are the Organizing Patterns of Interconnected Systems

Structures are the way a congregation, as an interrelated living system, has organized itself and its constituent parts. The metaphor is a living organism, which has boundaries and constituent parts that play important roles in keeping the organism alive. Such self-organization serves two purposes. It allows the congregation to maintain the integrity of its identity, and it also enables it to adapt and change in response to inner development and outside stimuli.[5] Although looking at structures appears to be a mechanical approach to the congregation, in fact structures remind leaders that everything is connected and that the system is designed to adapt and change in healthy ways.[6] Structures are also a political reality for a

---

5. Margaret Wheatley, *Finding Our Way: Leadership for an Uncertain Time* (San Francisco: Berrett-Koehler, 2005), 37.

6. Structural Family Theorist Salvador Minuchin, in Salvador Minuchin, Wai-Yung Lee, and George M. Simon, *Mastering Family Therapy: Journeys of Growth and Transformation* (New York: John Wiley & Sons, 1996), 30–31, wrote: "In truth there is no such thing as a family structure. Family structure is only a frame the therapist imposes on the data she observes. We think a therapist has to have a framework that offers a way of organizing and thinking about the great bustling, booming family world.... Nevertheless, I have found structural constructions useful. Designed to be heuristic and clinically suggestive, they help the therapist organize her perceptions and thinking in ways that lead to useful interventions. They also organize the therapist's observations of transactions, as well as verbal material."

congregation, providing order for power and authority. A structural assessment always includes a critique of the relative equality and inclusiveness of a particular structural pattern.[7] When the structures no longer serve the organization by helping it adapt to changes, the system either becomes inflexible and stuck or falls apart into chaos.[8] In other words, structures help focus on order instead of chaos in a living system. Thinking about boundaries, patterns, roles, triangles, and coalitions helps leaders regulate rampant anxiety in themselves and in the system.

Stories Are the Patterns of Meaning in a Community

The stories a congregation tells about itself are never just stories. Beyond its organizational structure, a congregation is a living system that has consciousness.[9] Humans are meaning-making creatures, and human systems are shaped around the existential patterns of meaning.[10] Stories are the outcropping of the existential consciousness of a congregation. They are also the ways God's truth is articulated in a community. They are not "just stories." Listening to stories helps a leader to interpret the patterns of heart of a congregation.[11] The mood, plots, types, and characters in the stories reveal relative health and the desire for health. The act of listening has a healing potential for the living system. A leader's appreciative ear for strengths and pockets of health encourages the members of a congregation to listen to their own stories and find hope where they had only known despair.

7. This is informed by the feminist/liberationist theology of Carter Heyward, _Saving Jesus from Those Who Are Right: Rethinking What It Means to Be Christian_ (Minneapolis: Fortress Press, 1999), 39–41. Heyward organizes her theological reflection in three areas that I interpret as corresponding to the three areas of assessment in this approach to church conflict. Looking at structures is a way of political knowledge, listening to stories relates to meaning as an existential form of knowledge, and learning from symptoms taps the deeper spiritual knowledge of the mystery of God at work.

8. Minuchin and others, _Mastering Family Therapy_, 32.

9. David Bohm, _Wholeness and the Implicate Order_ (London: Ark Books, 1980), 196.

10. Heyward, _Saving Jesus from Those Who Are Right_, 40.

11. James Hopewell, _Congregation: Stories and Structures_ (Minneapolis: Fortress, 1987).

Symptoms Are Responses to God's Work of Transformation

If structures are the material ordering of the life of a church, and stories are the spiritual articulation of its mind, symptoms are evidence of the process of time and change working on the congregation as a living organism. No creature of earth is immune to the changes of time. Each congregation is differently able to meet time's challenges. The need to hold on to identity[12] prompts some church members and leaders to resist change and the discomfort and losses it brings. The fear of chaos and uncertainty of the future discourage the risks of change. Love for the traditions and for the mothers and fathers of the congregation who passed that tradition down seems to suggest that change would mean disloyalty.[13] In such human needs, congregations get stuck with inadequate forms and practices. They fail to see that doing things "the way we always did" leads to death and not to life. Attention to the symptoms of conflict helps identify the resistance, the fear, the attachment, and the stuckness for their expected and forgivable humanness. The presence of symptoms drives the leader to a deeper spiritual knowing toward the mystery of God's transforming power at work in the congregation.[14]

Finding God's Wisdom in Interconnectedness

The strategies of looking at structures, listening to stories, and learning from symptoms work because they access the two deeper truths about how human systems function — interconnectedness and transformation. The first truth is that a congregation can best be understood as an organic, interconnected whole, an eco-system, or an emotional network in which all the parts are connected in circles of relationship.

---

12. Wheatley, *Finding Our Way,* 38.
13. Ronald Heifetz and Marty Linsky, *Leadership on the Line: Staying Alive through the Dangers of Leading* (Cambridge, MA: Harvard Business School Press, 2002), 28.
14. Heyward, *Saving Jesus from Those Who Are Right,* 41.

Congregations Are Interconnected Systems

An example from my youth helps me make sense of this truth. My father and I camped in a log cabin and hiked and hunted in an area of southern Illinois we called the Big Ponds. With shallow, smelly, muddy water, this swamp was a haven for beaver and waterfowl, and the woods around it were great for hunting mushrooms and hickory nuts. As far as we were concerned that's all it was. Today, of course, we know such swamps as wetlands, and we know that they are connected with the health and flexibility of a larger interconnected system called the Mississippi River basin. Wetlands play an important part in the water purity of the entire system, and an equally important part in the natural flood control on the rivers in that system.

Over the years, the Mississippi basin has experienced many changes. Levees have been built to protect towns along the riverbanks. Wetlands like the Big Ponds have been drained for farms and industrial use. As a result, the overall health of the whole system has suffered.

The repeated flooding of the Mississippi River over the last ten years and the disaster in New Orleans from hurricanes Katrina and Rita in the fall of 2005 are very much like church conflicts. The immediate effects of destruction and suffering are obvious, but it takes special eyes to see how larger changes have prompted the system to respond in unhealthy ways. Appropriating natural areas for commercial uses, including habitat for human beings, has crippled the drainage system's ability to adapt and absorb the extremes of weather.

The connection between the Big Ponds in southern Illinois and the levees of New Orleans is a real one. It's not a straight-line connection of cause and effect. Rather the relation is more complex. In a way the drainage system "wants" to circle back to its old ways when change happens. Manufactured levees and houses built on swampy ground are often no match for the natural forces of change on the whole system. The twin messages are that what happens in one part of the system affects the entire system and that the mysterious creative processes of God's creation are at work and powerful.

A congregation is an interconnected ecological system, much like a great waterway. Every small part of the system plays a role in the overall health and balance of the larger whole, and a change in any subsystem, however minor or apparently inconsequential, is felt throughout the system. Whether we look at the choir, or the missions committee, or even at some of the households or families of members of the church, they all are connected in relationships to the entire congregation. All of the changes in the choir's life, the failure of the missions committee to function, and any series of traumas in the lives of member families reverberate throughout the system and shift the balance and the health of the whole.

Interconnectedness and Resistance to Change

Understanding how everything is interrelated helps to make sense of how human institutions resist change. Because everything in a church is connected in delicate ecological balance, the smallest deviation from the usual balance is detected by parts of the congregation and, like an immune system, the church sets out to quarantine that change and minimize its effect. In a church, the phrase "we've never done it that way before" is an indicator of the resistance to change of a connected system. The balance of a complex system is often called homeostasis, and the person or unit that plays a key role in detecting and reacting to changes is called the "homeostat" (see "Characters in Church Narratives" on page 64 above). The truth of interrelatedness demonstrates how hard it is to bring about change in the church.

Change and Hope

At the same time, the truth of interrelatedness also shows how the process of change leads to hope. Every created thing is subject to change. Humans live in an ecological system on the planet earth that is constantly in transformation. The earth is itself a member of an ecological system revolving around a small star that is part of a galactic system in constant flux. Life is a process of growth and transformation. The Greek philosophers who imagined an ideal reality that was excused from the transitory nature of earth set the human race on a futile search for permanence. Philosophers of the twentieth century finally conceded that permanence does not exist and that change is the basic "stuff" of the cosmos. The human body is itself an ecological system in constant flux. The cells in the fingers touching my keyboard right now are in process of renewing themselves through death and rebirth. Any part of my body that is not constantly changing by taking in energy and sloughing off old matter is, in fact, dying.

A congregation is a living system facing constant change as well. Not only do members and leaders come and go and babies are born and folks get sick and die; the members and leaders are growing and changing, moving through developmental phases of their own lives with marriages and births and job changes and graduations and divorces and retirements. Further, the congregation itself is moving through developmental changes from its own birth and youth and periods of strength and times of change and decline. Finally, the congregation is buffeted by changes in its larger systems of communities and denominations and societies. Each of these changes calls for the risk of making adjustments in the balance of health and mission. While the people playing the role of homeostats call the church to hold on to the good old ways of doing things, the forces of change keep calling for newer ways. The trick is to hold on to the basic identity and integrity of the congregation while trying on new beliefs, practices, and organizational structures.

Finding God's Transforming Power

Change not only brings with it loss and grief; it also requires individuals as well as churches to be new creatures and to try new ways. The second truth about how congregations work is the assurance of God's transforming power. We can find hope in conflict because God is in charge and is pulling the world toward the new and the good. God is present in each moment when creativity is entertained, when novelty and growth are welcomed, when truth is greeted, when differences are appreciated, when community is celebrated.[15] Part of the mystery of conflict is the mysterious work of the Spirit of God to move a congregation — your congregation — toward something new and better. To be able to find hope in conflict, a leader — in this case, you — needs to be able to see the working of God in the tempests and turmoil of change.

Seeing the Working of God in Change

Looking back afterward, we see that transforming power was evident in the life of Richland Church, located in a changing neighborhood of a large northern city. Once a proud and vibrant congregation of European Americans from that neighborhood, the Richland area changed over the years from white middle class to African American working- and poverty-class residents. Members of the congregation responded to the turmoil of change with renewal efforts, opening a community center and youth outreach program that successfully served the needs of the neighborhood. These changes prompted some members to leave the church because of the change those renewal programs represented. As other members drifted into other congregations and many got older and could no longer participate in the life of the congregation, attendance and the church rolls dwindled to a breaking point of viability. The congregation faced a difficult choice between two alternatives: try one more renewal effort to attract new members from the neighborhood, or simply close their doors.

The debate raged for months within the congregation. At some points it looked as if a third alternative would emerge — that the congregation would split and effectively die from conflict. At some point in the debates however a new idea began to take shape. Knowing that the denomination had begun to explore the possibility of starting a new African American congregation in that neighborhood, one of the older members began talking about the possibility of donating the Richland church building to that project.

---

15. Henry Nelson Wieman, *Seeking a Faith for a New Age: Essays on the Interdependence of Religion, Science and Philosophy* (Metuchen, NJ: Scarecrow Press, 1975), 290.

As discussion continued, that idea grew in the imagination of members. After a few more months, the leaders had begun conversations with the denomination's leaders and a strategy began to emerge. Finally the denominational judicatory and the congregation adopted a plan that was beyond renewal for Richland Church. It was transformative.[16] The building and the church's leaders would be an incubator for a new congregation with a new African American church planting pastor. Today that building is home to a thriving new congregation thanks to the openness of the leaders of Richland Church to the transforming guidance of the Spirit of God.

Thinking Theologically about God and Change

Admittedly, that kind of transformation does not happen frequently. It is even hard for Christians to imagine that God can be part of the changes that they experience in the world. Instead, a lot of Christian thinking about God has preferred metaphors of permanence. The old hymn "Immortal, Invisible, God Only Wise" reinforces that preference. The words portray a transcendent, unchanging deity who needs nothing, not even rest, to rule the universe.

That mode of thinking plays on the human desire for permanence by mistaking infinity in its transcendent distance as the unchanging ideal. It seems to me this is a problem of perspective. Just as an airplane flying high above, traveling near the speed of sound, appears to move very slowly across the sky, so the infinite transcendence of God looks like a still-point from our ever-changing perspective.

A group of theologians of the twentieth century encouraged the Christian church to understand and trust the transformative power of God. So-called process theologians teach that God is changing and is the source of the complex processes of the universe. A look at the way the Hebrew Scriptures describe God — as relational, loving, volatile, changing God's mind from compassion to a hardened heart and back again — shows the flaw in assuming an unchanging God

---

16. Insight on transformation as a way through difficulties can be found in Robert E. Quinn, *Change the World: How Ordinary People Can Accomplish Extraordinary Results* (San Francisco: Jossey-Bass, 2000).

is the God of the Bible.[17] God appears to Job not as a still point of calm but in the whirlwind (Job 38:1; 40:1) and to Elijah along with tempest, earthquake, fire, and even silence (1 Kings 19:11).[18] God is more faithfully imagined as introducing something new and challenging to humankind than reinforcing what has been.[19] Jesus proclaimed a coming realm of God that was very different from the old kingdoms previously known.

These process theologians show us that we can count on God, not to stay the same, but to provide the possibility of change in every moment. In other words, the constant is change, not constancy. Once we get over the shock of a changing God, the thought can be very comforting. Our experience of life is one of constant change and challenge. Many of those changes are moving the world toward destruction rather than good. But God is out there in front of us in the vanguard of change, anticipating, calling us forward, onward, nudging us gently, and sometimes shaking us from our comfortable homeostasis. God stirs the waters to challenge us to the possibilities and opportunities beyond what we have thought or imagined.

Implications for Leadership

One lesson of the theology of transformation is that no leader can control the process of a congregation for very long. Your congregation as a living system will need to have its own interconnected mechanisms to hold on to its identity and stability in the face of change. If vicious circles of destructive change take hold (known to be destructive if they lead to less knowledge, less diversity, less community, and less ability to take mutual action), the congregation will need some of its own inner wisdom to stop runaway destructive behavior. For example, Antioch Church and Mission Church both needed someone to play a corrective role by saying, "We don't treat

17. Daniel Day Williams, *The Spirit and the Forms of Love* (New York: Harper & Row, 1968), 16–33.

18. Kyle Pasewark and Jeff Pool, eds. *The Theology of Langdon Gilkey: Systematic and Critical Studies* (Macon, GA: Mercer University Press, 1999), chapter 9.

19. John B. Cobb, *Reclaiming the Church: Where the Mainline Church Went Wrong and What to Do About It* (Louisville: Westminster John Knox Press, 1997).

our pastor that way in this church." Some mutual consent on the part of the congregation would have to acknowledge the normative authority of that statement to call members to accountability. Accountability is truthfulness in the organizational context.[20] When members are unwilling to be leaders who take the risk of standing up to destructive behavior, they allow the vicious cycles to continue.

However, control by itself, without the possibility for the system to accept change, embrace chaos, and engage in the mutual process of self-organization after transformation, can also lead to the death of an organization or a system.

As the leader in your congregation's conflict, you are one who can use hope and wisdom to trust and promote change. As the connections of relationship and emotion function or fail to function, as the turbulence sets in, you are at your best as a leader if you can avoid the temptation to jump in and be the savior-hero in the situation. Such behavior can actually short-circuit any change process and play right into the hands of resistance to change. From the other side of change, a leader who is rooting for needed change is wise to avoid taking too strong a stand to push the change faster than the system is ready to accept it. Founding Pastor Rob at Endwell Community Church (chapter 4) became anxious about the church's future and threw himself onto the wheel of change, trying to create a sense of renewal or transformation. His efforts seemed only to reinforce the balancing function that kept things the same as they had been.

The theology of transformation (change) suggests that the most effective roles of the leader in change are:

+ a careful observer who notes publicly what's happening without either fearing or prescribing the outcome.

+ a calm holder of verities, naming the truth of the current and emerging patterns without judgment or anxiety, perhaps opening a despairing story to hope.[21]

---

20. Hugh Halverstadt, *Managing Church Conflict* (Louisville: Westminster John Knox Press, 1991).

21. Andrew Lester, *Hope in Pastoral Care and Counseling* (Louisville: Westminster John Knox Press, 1995), 103.

◆ a "perturber"[22] who risks setting change in motion by prudently nudging, suggesting, proposing, framing and reframing stories, and challenging symptoms.

Radical Mutuality

Leading your congregation — especially in times of conflict — is best handled with a high degree of mutuality. In fact, I propose that we label this a "radical mutuality"[23] to describe the extent of the partnership between you, the leader, and other leaders and members and the partnership between the leader and God. It is radical because it goes against the grain of traditional leadership, which is about command and control,[24] and calls for more trust in partners in the work and more trust in the process of the organization as a living organism. Even for the times when heroic intervention may be needed and the situations when a direct authoritative action may be indicated, these decisions are made with the consent and wisdom of the group or organization behind them, not unilaterally nor from some higher authority. Only a radical mutuality takes full advantage of the deep connections of the congregation as a living organism. Only a radical mutuality can work in partnership with the transforming power of God. The mystery of conflict calls for the mutuality of leadership.

---

22. Dorothy Stroh Becvar and Raphael J. Becvar, *Family Therapy: A Systemic Integration* (Boston: Allyn and Bacon, 2000), 110.

23. A convergence of insights on mutuality has led me to use this term. Carter Heyward writes that "mutuality is the creative basis of our lives, the world, and God. It is the dynamic of our life together in the world insofar as we are fostering justice and compassion. Moreover it is the constant wellspring of our power to make justice-love" (*Saving Jesus from Those Who Are Right*, 62). Meg Wheatley notes that leaders of corporations who have moved through difficult transitions not only change themselves, but they also "are supporting teams, fostering collaboration and more participative processes, introducing new ways of thinking. They are setting a great many things in motion simultaneously within the organization. Some work, some don't, but the climate for experimentation is evident. A change here elicits a response there, which calls for a new idea, which elicits yet another response. It's an intricate exchange and coevolution, and it's nearly impossible to look back and name any single change as the cause of all the others. In this way organizational change is a dance, not a forced march" (*Finding Our Way*, 72–73).

24. Wheatley, *Finding Our Way*, 64ff.

The pains and griefs of conflict present themselves as a mystery, confusing and befuddling even the best of us. The mystery is often shrouded by high emotions and presenting issues that distract our attention from the deeper, truer realities of the situation. When we stop to ask ourselves what is at the heart of this situation, when we listen with our full attention to the music in the background, when we open our hearts without holding back to transcend the sense of being stuck in helplessness, then we will find the keys to unlock the mystery of conflict. Seeing the interconnectedness of the congregation as a community opens us to the possibility of genuine, loving, mutual resolution. Acknowledging the reality of change and the presence of God out ahead of us in that change prompts us to trust in hope and let a congregation move through its difficulties in its own unique and wise ways. The keys to the mystery of church conflict work because they are grounded in these understandings of community and change.

Reflection on the Mystery of Conflict

1. Take some quiet time for yourself in which you set aside your usual problem-solving techniques and open yourself to your congregation as a living, dynamic, organic unity. Wait for that moment in which the whole comes into view.

2. If question 1 is difficult for you, choose some of the readings in the bibliography, particularly Ronald Richardson, *Creating a Healthier Church*, or Frank Thomas, *Spiritual Maturity* (on seeing congregations as systems), or Peter Senge, *The Fifth Discipline*, or Margaret Wheatley, *Finding Our Way* (on seeing secular organizations as systems). As you read, seek a new way of seeing.

3. Write a paragraph on what you believe about God's involvement in your congregation, particularly in this time of conflict. Is God distant and unchanging or present and engaged in transforming individuals and congregations? What does God desire of your congregation and of you?

4. What is your present or accustomed role in your congregation's present conflict: Hero/savior? Victim? Identified problem? Helper? Reactor? Homeostat? See "Characters in Church Narratives" on page 64 for definitions. What do you need to do to shift your role toward that of leader? How can you become a calm observer? A holder of verities? A perturber?

5. If your congregation is not currently in a conflict situation, how can you use the keys presented here to create a healthier congregation and prevent future destructive conflict?

Conclusion

On Being a
Careful, Reflective Leader

*Rather than think of ourselves as change agents, [o]ur goal is
to perturb the system in such a way that it compensates with
more functional behaviors for the system. In other words, we
must provide new information, which the system may choose
to incorporate into a self-corrective process that at the same
time facilitates self-maintenance.*
— Dorothy Stroh Becvar and Raphael J. Becvar[1]

George Carlin plays an innovative Roman Catholic bishop in the
movie *Dogma*. He plans a bold intervention to update the church's
image with a new statue of the "Buddy Christ" with thumbs up, and
to offer a day of amnesty in which all sins are forgiven. Typical of
many church leaders, however, he is bigger on ideas of what should
be done than he is on listening and learning. When he is told of
a serious flaw in his plan (in which all creation will be destroyed
if two fallen angels enter the church and receive forgiveness, thus
negating, according to the logic of the film, God's eternal decree),
he refuses to hear and moves ahead with his intervention. Much
bloodshed and terror results and only a direct appearance of God
(herself) is able to save creation!

I can identify with Carlin's bishop. I have personally served in
situations of responsibility and, without sufficient attention to the
keys to the mystery of the situation, have offered bold interventions

---

1. Dorothy Stroh Becvar and Raphael J. Becvar, *Family Therapy: A Systemic
Integration* (Boston: Allyn and Bacon, 2000), 110.

that I was sure would fix the conflict and save the congregation. I have also stood helplessly by to watch leaders and committees and consultants who thrust ahead with bold solutions to congregational problems with little reflection on the culture, the context, or the power dynamics involved.

I have written this book because I want to encourage all of us who are leaders to open our eyes, our ears, and our hearts to the complexity and hopefulness of congregational conflict and be extra careful and reflective before attempting our interventions.

One way of articulating my concern is to offer the ethical motto of the medical profession: "First, do no harm." These words remind the helping professional to be humble in the practice of caring for others, recognizing the potential for gaps in knowledge and errors of judgment.

For a church leader, these words stand as a reminder that a congregation is an interconnected whole with its own life and identity. To intervene in a way that might dictate a solution in some authoritarian way does harm to the integrity of the congregation as a whole. Often, for example, leaders or consultants recommend removal of a pastor or other staff member without acknowledging how change or stress or despair has led the congregation to project the anxieties of the situation onto that person as the identified problem. Of course there are sometimes persons in a congregation, perhaps even pastors or staff members, who have acted in ways that are destructive of the advancement of health and faith in the congregation. Careful attention to structures, stories, and symptoms will help distinguish whether the issue is individual mischief or system-wide turbulence. Ordinarily, however, the congregation is harmed by the approach that suggests all the problems will be resolved by removing the "broken" part of the congregational machine and replacing it with a different one.

The radical mutuality suggested in the previous chapter offers a strategy for avoiding harm. Helping a congregation to find their own wisdom, strength, health, and hope with which to address their problems is far preferable. Using the three keys of this method, doing no harm might mean:

◆ *Structural inconsistencies or inequities can be named without requiring a "right" structural solution.* In the Big Bluff City Church, the consultants introduced the church board to the denominational constitution as an educational opportunity. The board members themselves enthusiastically embraced those formal structures as a helpful approach to their problems.

◆ *Suggesting alternate, more hopeful stories leaves a congregation free to interpret them as they choose.* When he found himself unclear about what to do to help a family, family therapist Ray Becvar used to simply pull a random story from his memory and tell his clients to go home and think about it. Invariably, he said, the family would begin the next session with the declaration, "We know why you gave us that story to think about."[2] It would be the family's own construction of pattern and meaning that brought the learning, not the direct intervention of the therapist.

◆ *The symptoms are only metaphors for the connectedness and transformation experienced by the congregation.* The only harmless and humble intervention regarding symptoms is to challenge them or to call attention to their metaphorical nature. The high emotions, the projections, the distancing, the protection of secrets all are real and worthy of attention, but they are not to be addressed and treated. In the anxiety to alleviate suffering, the leader is always tempted to manipulate the congregation to remove the symptom. When a congregation is intent on "firing" an "identified problem" pastor, forbidding them to do so only energizes the congregation to hold on to or even escalate their loyalty to their symptoms because they prefer the pain they know to the pain they do not know. One member of our conflict team would tell such a congregation that they had every right to recommend that the pastor be removed, and that they should know that the conflict team would simply send a recommendation against it to the regional judicatory. That allowed for a free choice. Rather than face a fight at the judicatory level, the board or committee

---

2. Information given in a seminar for the Certificate in Family Therapy, St. Louis Family Institute, Spring 1991.

usually preferred to try again to mediate a solution that was more complex. Encouraging leaders and members to choose healthier alternative behaviors leaves the freedom to change to the congregation and leaves the direction of the change to the transforming spirit of God.

Serving as a teacher or a perturber or a challenger is often a way to avoid doing harm in a conflict setting. On the other hand, the imperative to "do no harm" is not to be confused with "avoid all pain." Often leaders decline to act for a variety of reasons. Often the reason is to avoid the pain or suffering that might come from taking a clear, loving, and hopeful position in a conflicted situation. Avoiding pain and suffering is a way of underfunctioning as a leader. When the spirit of God helps me see something and I fail to respond, I am neglecting the creative power of God. The arguments against "avoiding all pain" are summarized by the three keys of this work.

- Stories without pain hold little truth.

- Ignoring structural inequities reinforces the resistance to change in the way the congregation has organized itself.

- If God wants something to happen and the symptoms are signs of the resistance or avoidance of that desire, to accept symptoms is to thwart the will of God.

So being careful and being reflective are not simple tasks for you as a leader of a congregation in conflict. But they are practices that are possible to learn and that make a difference. They are worthy because the church, including the congregations that make up the church universal, is an institution worthy of good leadership. Of course it has its human frailties, and it often has been led in ways that lean away from health. But it is the appointed community of the transforming power of God in Jesus Christ. I invite you to listen to the call to become a leader who will discern the movement of God within your congregation and help the church universal move forward into God's good future.

Bibliography

Becvar, Dorothy Stroh, and Raphael J. Becvar. *Family Therapy: A Systemic Integration*. Boston: Allyn and Bacon, 2000.

Benyei, Candace R. *Understanding Clergy Misconduct in Religious Systems: Scapegoating, Family Secrets and the Abuse of Power*. New York: Haworth Press, 1998.

Bergman, Joel. *Fishing for Barracuda: Pragmatics of Brief Systemic Therapy*. New York: W. W. Norton, 1985.

Bohm, David. *Wholeness and the Implicate Order*. London: Ark Books, 1980.

Borg, Marcus. *Meeting Jesus Again for the First Time*. New York: Harper-Collins, 1994.

Bowen, Murray. *Family Therapy in Clinical Practice*. Northvale, NJ: Jason Aronson, 1986.

Branson, Mark L. *Memories, Hopes and Conversations: Appreciative Inquiry and Congregational Change*. Bethesda, MD: Alban Institute, 2004.

Brown, Raymond E. *The Churches the Apostles Left Behind*. Mahwah, NJ: Paulist Press, 1984.

Brueggemann, Walter. *Theology of the Old Testament*. Minneapolis: Fortress Press, 1997.

Carse, James P. *Finite and Infinite Games: A Vision of Life as Play and Possibility*. New York: Ballantine, 1986.

Cobb, John B. *Reclaiming the Church: Where the Mainline Church Went Wrong and What to Do about It*. Louisville: Westminster John Knox Press, 1997.

Cosgrove, Charles H., and Dennis D. Hatfield. *Church Conflict: The Hidden Systems behind the Fights*. Nashville: Abingdon, 1994.

Dykstra, Craig. *Growing in the Life of Faith: Education and Christian Practices*. Louisville: Geneva Press, 1999.

Everist, Norma Cook. *Church Conflict*. Nashville: Abingdon Press, 2004.

Friedman, Edwin. *Generation to Generation*. New York: Guilford, 1985.

Goodrich, Thelma Jean, et al. *Feminist Family Therapy: A Casebook*. New York: Norton, 1988.

Groome, Thomas. *Sharing Faith: A Comprehensive Approach to Religious Education and Pastoral Ministry, the Way of Shared Praxis.* San Francisco: HarperSanFrancisco, 1991.

Halverstadt, Hugh F. *Managing Church Conflict.* Louisville: Westminster John Knox, 1991.

Heifetz, Ronald A., and Marty Linsky. *Leadership on the Line: Staying Alive through the Dangers of Leading.* Cambridge, MA: Harvard Business School Press, 2002.

Heyward, Carter. *Saving Jesus from Those Who Are Right: Rethinking What It Means to Be Christian.* Minneapolis: Fortress Press, 1999.

Hoffman, Lynn. *Foundations of Family Therapy: A Conceptual Framework for Systems Change.* New York: Basic Books, 1981.

Hopewell, James. *Congregation: Stories and Structures.* Minneapolis: Fortress, 1987.

James, P. D. *The Lighthouse.* London: Faber and Faber, 2005.

Kingsolver, Barbara. *High Tide in Tucson: Essays from Now or Never.* New York: HarperPerennial, 1995.

Leas, Speed. *Discover Your Conflict Management Style.* Rev. ed. Bethesda, MD: Alban Institute, 1997.

Lerner, Harriet G. *The Dance of Anger.* New York: Harper and Row, 1985.

Lester, Andrew D. *Hope in Pastoral Care and Counseling.* Louisville: Westminster John Knox Press, 1995.

Madanes, Cloe. *Sex, Love and Violence.* New York: Norton, 1990.

Minuchin, Salvador. *Families and Family Therapy.* Cambridge, MA: Harvard University Press, 1974.

———. *Family Healing: Strategies for Hope and Understanding.* New York: Free Press, 1993.

———. "Where Is the Family in Narrative Family Therapy?" *Journal of Marital and Family Therapy* 24, no. 4 (1998): 397–418.

Minuchin, Salvador, and Charles H. Fishman. *Family Therapy Techniques.* Cambridge, MA: Harvard University Press, 1981.

Minuchin, Salvador, and Michael P. Nichols. *Family Healing: Strategies for Hope and Understanding.* New York: Free Press, 1998.

Minuchin, Salvador, Wai-Yung Lee, and George M. Simon. *Mastering Family Therapy: Journeys of Growth and Transformation.* New York: John Wiley & Sons, 1996.

Mitchell, Kenneth R. *Multiple Staff Ministries.* Louisville: Westminster, 1988.

Morgan, Donn F. *The Making of Sages: Biblical Wisdom and Contemporary Culture.* Harrisburg, PA: Trinity Press International, 2002.

Papp, Peggy. *The Process of Change.* New York: Guilford, 1983.

Pasewark, Kyle, and Jeff Pool, eds. *The Theology of Langdon Gilkey: Systematic and Critical Studies.* Macon, GA: Mercer University Press, 1999.

Pauw, Amy Plantinga. "The Church as a Community of Gift and Argument." Unpublished work in progress, 2002.

Quinn, Robert E. *Change the World: How Ordinary People Can Accomplish Extraordinary Results.* San Francisco: Jossey-Bass, 2000.

Ragsdale, Katherine, ed. *Boundary Wars: Intimacy and Distance in Healing Relationships.* Cleveland: Pilgrim Press, 1996.

Rediger, Lloyd. *Clergy Killers: Guidance for Pastors and Congregations under Attack.* Louisville: Westminster John Knox Press, 1997.

Richardson, Ronald W. *Becoming a Healthier Pastor.* Minneapolis: Fortress, 2004.

———. *Creating a Healthier Church: Family Systems Theory, Leadership, and Congregational Life.* Minneapolis: Fortress, 1996.

Rushdie, Salman. *Haroun and the Sea of Stories.* New York: Penguin Books, 1990.

Sachs, Jonathan. *The Dignity of Difference: How to Avoid the Clash of Civilizations.* London: Continuum Books, 2002.

Satir, Virginia. "A Partial Portrait of a Family Therapist in Process." In *Evolving Models for Family Change: A Volume in Honor of Salvador Minuchin,* ed. H. Charles Fishman and Bernice Rosman, 278–93. New York: Guilford Press, 1986.

Sawyer, David R. *Work of the Church: Getting the Job Done in Boards and Committees.* Valley Forge, PA: Judson Press, 1986.

Schmidt, Frederick. *What God Wants for Your Life: Finding Answers to the Deepest Questions.* New York: HarperCollins, 2005.

Senge, Peter M. *The Fifth Discipline: the Art and Practice of the Learning Organization.* New York: Doubleday, 1990.

Senge, Peter, et al. *Presence: An Exploration of Profound Change in People, Organizations, and Society.* New York: Currency Books, 2004.

Southworth, Bruce. *At Home in Creativity: The Naturalistic Theology of Henry Nelson Wieman.* Boston: Skinner House Books, 1995.

Steinke, Peter. *Healthy Congregations.* Bethesda, MD: Alban Institute, 1996.

———. *How Your Church Family Works.* Bethesda, MD: Alban Institute, 1993.

Susek, Ron. *Firestorm: Preventing and Overcoming Church Conflicts.* Grand Rapids, MI: Baker Books, 1999.

Thomas, Frank A. *Spiritual Maturity: Preserving Congregational Health and Balance.* Minneapolis: Fortress, 2002.

Thomas, Marlin. *Resolving Disputes in Christian Groups.* Winnepeg: Windflower Communications, 1994.

Thompson, George, Jr. *How to Get Along with Your Church: Creating Cultural Capital for Doing Ministry.* Cleveland: Pilgrim Press, 2001.

Tillich, Paul. *Systematic Theology.* Vol. 1. Chicago: University of Chicago Press, 1951.

Wheatley, Margaret. *Finding Our Way: Leadership for an Uncertain Time.* San Francisco: Berrett-Koehler, 2005.

Wieman, Henry Nelson. *Seeking a Faith for a New Age: Essays on the Interdependence of Religion, Science and Philosophy.* Metuchen, NJ: Scarecrow Press, 1975.

Wiesel, Elie. *The Time of the Uprooted.* New York: Alfred Knopf, 2005.

Williams, Daniel Day. *The Spirit and the Forms of Love.* New York: Harper and Row, 1968.